What's It Mean – Shifting to Green?

Getting to the Finish Line

KATHRYN ALEXANDER

Resilient Planet Publishing
Spokane, Washington

RESILIENT PLANET PRESS

9116 E Sprague #585 Spokane, WA 99206
http://www.whatsitmeanshiftingtogreen.com

Kathryn Alexander. What's It Mean - Shifting To Green? Getting to the Finish Line Kindle Edition.

ISBN-10: 0615885721

ISBN-13: 978-0615885728

DEDICATION

This series is dedicated to the human species in the hope that we can begin to treasure what we value, trust and forgive ourselves, and act with courage on our convictions. We can do it — yes we can!

&

TABLE OF CONTENTS

ACKNOWLEDGMENTS

There are SO many who have contributed to this work! Ludwig von Bertalanffy – my first exposure to systems thinking and Béla H. Bánáthy and Peter Senge who deepened it, Jane Jacobs who open my eyes to values as systems, Janine Benyus, Thomas Berry, Michael Dowd, and Brian Swimm with their deep commitment to Earth. Bernard Lietaer and Edgar Cahn's economic insights and Nelson Mandela for showing what humanity can be. These are just the tips of iceberg!

∽

A GIFT FOR YOU

As a gift to you I'd like to offer you a free checklist. This checklist asks you questions about all three stages of sustainability. Answering these questions can offer insight and give you some indication of where you are (potentially surprising) and what you might do to fulfill all three stages.

Please visit this link:
http://whatsitmeanshiftingtogreen.com/checklist

Join us on Facebook at:
http://www.facebook.com/ethicalimpact

Follow us on Twitter at:
http://Twitter.com/ethicalimpact

Please – pay it forward by reviewing this book on Amazon Thank you!!!.

๛

How Should We Live?

As I look back over the history of the human race I see times and places of great experiments. In India the society was built around a search for internal knowing. The sacred texts of India, the Vedas, speak of their discoveries about our internal nature and how we are connected to the rest of creation. The Incas, most notably in

Machu Picchu, created an architecture that fit in within the environment in astonishing ways. The Mayan took astronomy to new heights. Each civilization had a specialty that expanded and deepened our knowledge about what it means to live on Planet Earth.

When we were few we had the luxury of tinkering with things and the damage we did was minimal and the resilience of nature restorative. Now that we are many, we need to integrate our dreams in a way that ensures continued life on a healthy planet.

The *how* of life forms the container for actions and choices that ensure the vigorous health of all, yet the container does not determine the content. We are forever free to choose the *what* of our lives, but the *how* has now become a global question. What kind of context can we create that does not interfere with the various belief systems that give people hope and identity? What approach to life can be universal and yet individual? Where can we look for guidance that will provide a shared experience? The only source I can see is nature, her self.

Nature is all about Life and abundance. She fosters life in every kind of situation and she's been getting better and better at it as life has become more and more complex, increasing in both kind and in number for the past 3.8 *billion* years. Surely she has something to teach us! Her patters, principles and yes values, are something every person can affirm from their own experience, if they so choose. Distilling the observations and insights of an army of curious individuals has begun to clarify just exactly how she does it so we can follow suit.

Science has been concerned with the what of nature, but it is only when you look at the *why* that so many of the seeming contradictions fall into place. This series of books is my contribution to this exploration. The two basic tenants of Mother Nature: all actions support the capacity for life, with the intention of maintaining the integrity of the whole, make every action she takes make sense. Not only that, by using these two main principles/values as the foundation for our own decision-making, we can begin to bring forth those same conditions.

Gandhi so famously said, "Be the change you want to see." We *want* a lush and healthy planet! We *want* a vibrant and abundant life! Who best to learn from about how to do that then the expert herself – Mother Nature. What better place to begin to practice this new way of being than business? In business we have small groups of people with a common purpose who are trying to achieve success. This is the *what*, becomes integrated with life using the *how* of sustainability – taking that journey all the way to the third stage. What an exhilarating prospect!

The Sustainable Values Set® is a work in progress. As we explore and question I have no doubt that it will become much more refined and clear. Understanding the systems dynamics that a system of values has, like any other system, is a new milestone in how we see ethics, values and integrity. We are moving from parts and pieces – an approach that has blinded us to the implications of our actions, to understanding wholes and their interrelationship. It is this shift that will allow us to make better decisions, see implications *before* damage is done, and allow us to maintain the integrity of our vision of a vibrant and healthy world for us all. Thinking differently is a road that takes courage *and* companionship.

It takes many eyes to see clearly through the fog of our misconceptions. Many, many people have started down this road already so we have tools and methods that allow us to begin to engage with what is emerging. We *are* the people we have been waiting for – and the time is NOW!

What's It Mean - Shifting To Green?

The word 'sustainable' means to be in existence for a long time on a continuous basis. We've done all right, so far, living on this big blue ball for about 5 million years, as a species. Think we have another 5 million? How about 10,000 years more, is that doable, do you think? That is the kind of 'sustainability' I'm talking about here. What do we have to do to ensure we can live, and live well, as a species on this most hospitable planet for the next 10,000 years?

The trouble is our belief in separation. We see ourselves and everything else as separate, a collection of parts and pieces. If we even stopped and thought for a moment we would know this isn't true, as life of any sort is not possible with out the contributions of lots of others (plants and animals come to mind). So it is this illusion that we need to eliminate.

Our current approach to sustainability is very much focused on seeing the Earth as a vast bank account and we are trying to balance our income and out go by reducing our wasteful use of resources. Great! We definitely need to reduce our spending habits, but that is only a small part of the picture. It helps to see sustainability as a journey and not a destination. The journey has three distinct parts.

The first stage is the one we have just entered. By reducing our use of finite resources then we gain time and vastly improve our processes. Waste is both uneconomical and unsustainable. It is also immoral, but more on that can be found in my other book, *Doing What's Right: Finding ethics in a sea of values.* Our current focus has to do with energy and some carbon. It is the release of carbon that is the most crucial. If we don't drastically reduce that we won't get to the next stages. However water is really a close second and a resource we waste in astronomical amounts. Take this quote from a recent article at www.forbes.com:

"In Tarrant County, Texas, <u>Ceres</u> found that fracking consumed 2.8 billion gallons in 2011, and that was only "about 10% of the water used in all of Texas for hydraulic fracturing."

That's an impressive and disturbing statistic—until you compare it with, say, the amount of water Texans dump onto their lawns. Folks in Fort Worth, Tarrant County's biggest city with a population of more than 750,000, used an average 6.8 billion gallons a year outside their residences from 2004 through 2011, according to the Texas Water Development Board, with 80% to 90% going onto lawns.

Nationwide, the EPA estimates that landscape irrigation consumes about nine billion gallons of water a day. That's more than three trillion gallons a year, or more than 20 times its highest estimate for the amount of water used annually in fracking."

In the article the percentages are used to *justify* not being concerned, as if 2.8 billion gallons was nothing, since we use more on laws, and then, while that's a bigger amount it's still just a drop in the bucket.... And so it goes. So yes, we still have a long way to go in just learning to manage our resources. Unilever and Proctor & Gamble are really good examples of progressive companies at this stage.

We have gotten so used to the Earth's ability to restore and refresh that we just *assume* she can continue to do that. The Theory of Constraints suggests otherwise. The Theory of Constraints says that the system functions at optimum capacity when the entire systems flow is regulated to the maximum flow of its biggest restriction. In a mechanical system if the bottleneck only allows for 18 parts an hour then everyone else must function at that same rate *even if they are capable of going twice as fast.* In living systems the restriction has to do with the rate of replacement. Oil, for instance, takes millions of years to replace. Got the picture?

The second stage has to do with beginning to actually learn and mimic Mother Nature. In nature there is NO waste, nada, zilch, nothing goes to waste. *Everything* is eaten, at some point and nothing is withheld from that process. When businesses begin to understand this and apply it, then not only do costs decline, but new income streams get discovered, clearly a win-win-win situation. And that the point, following nature's lead is a win for every one! In this stage we are beginning to understand the interdependence that lies at the heart of a healthy ecosystem and, at the same time, get handle on our role in making health possible. Interface Carpets, Inc. is a sterling example of a company working with great integrity in this area. They expect to achieve their goal of being carbon neutral in 2015. Visit the Zeri organization to see more case studies.

The third stage however is a quantum jump ahead. In the first stage we are still outside the system working on it, interacting is ways that focused on us – in a very human centric way. In the second stage we are becoming more in relationship with the Earth. We are beginning to understand the significance of how she works and the benefits of learning from her. In the third stage we become partners in her evolution. In the third stage we not only get out of her way and stop resisting what she wants to do, but we actively *facilitate* her wisdom, by working *with* her processes, principles and yes, values. Here is where the discipline we have been developing in the first two stages will really pay off as we gain insight into what actually works and what doesn't. Grupo Balbo in Sao Paulo, Brazil is an excellent example of a company that understands its role in all of the ecosystems it resides in.

This is the context in which to read this book. *True sustainability means that the Earth will celebrate our existence because we are able to partner in co-evolution, making both our lives and hers all the better for being here.* How can we make this happen?

&

1 Being Here Forever

Help people pull away from their current practice and beliefs and move into the new philosophy without a feeling of guilt about the past. ~ **W. Edwards Deming,** The New Economics

My Theory

I have a theory: 'a long time' is equal to the length of a lifetime, that means we can only see or even consider a span of time that is about 100 years, the length of our life. This shortsighted view makes forever seem like someone else's problem. I'd like us to begin to think about being on the planet for another 10, 000 years. That's really not so much since humanoids have been here for about 5 million years, but it looks impossible, given how much destruction we've been able to create in the past 200.

Think about it. It has taken us just 200 years to bring us to the edge of our 5,000,000-year sojourn. That's an astounding fact. We are witnessing the disappearance of millions of years of ice, ice that will never be replaced. Yet while we are awed by the spectacle, we are complacent about the implications. We cling to our habits, our denial, and our lack of responsibility as if they are badges of our importance. We can't seem to bring ourselves to believe that we are fallible, that we are at risk, and that we can - we have to forgive ourselves for what we have done if we want to change it. Can we do better? We *have* to do better!

Ecologically Sustainable - Is It Really Urgent?

I'm passionate about sustainability for many reasons. First and foremost I LOVE the planet, nature is a source of life to me. Secondly I'm more than excited about what rethinking business can do for business while doing good things for nature. Third, I like change. I really do! I see change as a creative edge that brings forth new possibilities and since I'm a variety junkie, change rocks!

For all of the reasons listed above I've had my antennae up around the issue of climate change for some time. Talk about depressing! Really looking at this issue and knowing what's coming is enough to drive anyone to drink.

I don't talk much about climate change because it can be so depressing. I'm not about putting my head in the sand, but you can only take so much, you know? That said, today I DO want to sound the alarm! View this video and get ready to recommit to the fight!

She's Alive... Beautiful... Finite... Hurting... Worth Dying for.

The planet IS worth saving! Our home IS worth saving! People we love and care for have died in this fight and many more will die before it's over, but *this* fight IS worth it! We have to remember though, that it is not just about fighting! THIS change is about possibilities! It is about a *new* way to live in harmony so we can have the time and sensitivity to enjoy nature and her bounty!

Harmony...Walter J. Stahel wrote a paper called the "Five Pillars of Sustainability" in the early 90s. He saw sustainability in the following ways:

- Pillar of nature conservation
- Pillar of limited toxicity

These form the domain of environmental protection:

- Pillar of Resource Productivity

These three form the basis of a sustainable economy:

- Pillar of Social Ecology
- Pillar of Cultural Ecology

The last two, however, are really what is meant by the "People Piece" of the Triple Bottom Line – People, Planet and Profit. Without peace we will continue to devastate the natural world and our own history and legacy as well. War is destructive - it destroys everything in its path. It is not sustainable. It never was, but now we destroy on such a scale and with such thoroughness that the damage is immense and it *must* be stopped.

We will only stop our squabbling when we learn to respect others and allow them to make decisions about their own future, with or without our input. We must evoke the inherent dignity and worth of every person, valuing their contributions and be willing to learn from them when we differ. This includes repairing the rift between genders. I support the Satyana Institute for just that reason. Until we respect and honor the feminine, we will not be able to respect and honor nature.

The stopping of war speaks to the fifth pillar – Culture, Ethics and Values. We are an amazing species - so willing to destroy that which we love. We rationalize it in all kinds of ways, but I have marveled at how often and how thoroughly we do it. Our rape of nature and women is testimony to it. Our destruction of the buildings and monuments that form our human legacy on this planet whose destruction is rationalized by war is a testament to it. That 20% of Colorado's children do not know where their next meal is coming from is also a testament to it. I could go on. We pay CEO's enormous sums and fuss about raising teacher's salaries. We do NOT honor what we claim to love. How different would the world be if we honored what we loved?

Sustainable Intelligence: Applying the Wisdom of Nature

The point of Sustainable Intelligence is to begin to think as nature does, thus benefiting from the insight she's gained over 3.8 billion years. One aspect of nature's thinking that offers insight is *permeability*. In chemistry this is most often seen in cell membranes that allow oxygen and proteins to flow through the cell membranes, thus nourishing our bodies. The physics is such that when there is more of something on one side and less on the other this imbalance causes the flow from one side to another.

In ecologies permeability is a bit different as the boundaries are not as distinct as they are with a cell. Here the sustainable value of dynamic stability comes into play. Dynamic Stability is vividly seen in nature through streams and rivers. Over time the water wears away the banks and the course changes. Very old rivers have very winding riverbeds. Yet, while major changes have taken place they have occurred through small changes that happened over time. In business this was expressed in the Total Quality Movement (TQM) by the idea of continuous improvement. If small incremental changes are made continuously, over time major change will happen, but without the effort, pain, risk and expense that results from large and sudden changes.

The idea of boundaries in ecologies however, is also a bit different. This is most clearly seen in the way we talk about forest growth. Evergreens grow in the mountains and as you move down in elevation the kind of tree changes into deciduous (oaks and maples etc.). There is no definite boundary where on one side are evergreens and on the other deciduous. That boundary is permeable, or said another way; there is a graduated range from one kind of tree to another.

This is how nature works - there are ranges rather than lines of demarcation between things. Your temperature is one such range. Very rarely do you have a temperature of 98.6°. If you wanted to keep it stable you'd spend the whole day putting on and taking off clothes. There is a range, from about 104/105 to 92 and both ends of this range are dangerous and lead to death.

This understanding can be applied to business in many interesting and productive ways. All processes have a range. Measure it and if the results of that process do not match your customer expectations, then you *change the process* so the *normal range* **does** give you the results you need.

This understanding also has a profound impact on how we understand cities. It is normal for us to think of 'infill' as the appropriate way to preserve the environment. What this results in however, is a solid block of concrete (consider New York) with occasional patches of green (in New York's case - one - Central Park). This solidity does not allow for any sort of dynamic balance or permeability. This suggests that we need to rethink our city model as we move towards 'green cities'.

Thinking sustainably, using sustainable intelligence, means that we think in terms of wholes rather than parts, thus seeking to ensure the health of the whole, by mitigating and managing impact for the long-term instead of the short-term.

We've walled off nature and decreed 'nature free' zones in many areas, from agriculture and animal raising to eliminating insect habitat to even managing the climate in our buildings. In small areas and when we were few, the impacts seemed negligible. Now that we are many and globally interconnected, the impact is profound with extreme and unintended consequences.

We need to welcome nature back in, swallow our discomfort, tolerate the inconvenience and pay more attention to what we love and less to what we hate.

Growth – the Holy Grail of the 21st Century

Everything is predicated on growth. The economy *must* grow. Every business *must* grow. You have to grow or you're going backwards, you can't stand still! It's all about doing more, selling more, and having more locations than last year. Really?

Maybe we could grow instead in skill, wisdom, compassion and creativity. Maybe we could grow in innovation, in harmony with each other and nature; maybe we could grow in sophistication, in caring, and in generosity. Maybe.

Maybe we could evolve…what would that look like? Would we need more stuff? Would we need to have bigger buildings, bigger bank accounts, bigger market share? What would it look like if we chose evolution instead of growth?

What would happen if we all slowed down? One of the major drivers for growth is interest from loans. Interest *requires* that you have more money than you borrowed to pay back the loan. If you don't grow – you go in the hole. This is one reason why usury has been forbidden by every religion. Hummm…, wonder what would happen if we went to 3% interest or even 1%?

I know this all sounds like wishful thinking, but we have *got* to do something. To see what some others are saying take a gander at this. This is a trailer for the movie "Hooked on Growth" Growth is something we *must* get a handle on, or else we are chasing disaster.

We need to rethink what really excites us, what makes life meaningful. It's not more stuff. If we can withstand the pressure of growing, if we can stop running for running's sake and act only when it makes us supremely happy, if we can tune in to what we *really* want – and not settle for second best, then the concept of growth will look completely different.

If we can begin to think better instead of bigger, then we just might have a chance!

Reciprocity

Dassault Systèmes President and CEO Bernard Charlès sums it up simply: "What a company takes from the planet's resources to create and deliver a product must be surpassed by the value that product or service delivers to the people it serves." according (Fall 2012 issue of Contact Magazine). What's wrong with this picture?

Actually several things, first it is human centric. It is a form of "the ends justify the means." Most of our human centric focus carries the same kind of thinking. If it is good for humans then that justifies the death and destruction of anything else. Tar sands anyone?

Secondly, "taking" is a one-way street. That kind of action is desecration, pure and simple. This is the problem that is at the heart of sustainability – taking. The natural world functions as well as it does and for as long as it has (3.8 billion years) *because* there is NO taking. Taking is *unsustainable*! Nature functions from the value of reciprocity.

All ecosystems function from the foundation of reciprocity. Reciprocity is about giving and receiving, not about taking and manipulation, not about power grabs, but mutual support. Reciprocity ensures that both or all parties get what they need and that the health of the whole is paramount.

In nature the health of the ecosystem
requires the health of all. No species lives at the
expense of another species – except us humans.
Nature is distributive, only humans have designed
systems that serve a few of the species at the
expense of the rest. This habit of supporting a few
at the expense of the rest is showing the cracks of
its un-sustainability (as evidenced by the
continuing economic crises).

If the products Dassault Systèmes makes
are non-polluting – great, if there are no toxins in
those products or in the making of those products
then great. If there is no waste generated in the
making and selling of those products – better. But
until there is a giving back, a restoring to the
Earth of what was taken, they are not sustainable
then they are not regenerative.

Give a Hand to P&G – A Green Business Company?

I was on a call press release today with
Proctor and Gamble (P&G). They were sharing
their 20/20 goals for sustainability. They should
be applauded for their commitment to energy
reduction: 30% reduction in energy use using

renewables, 20% reduction in packaging and 20% decrease in water use. Great reductions given that they just started on this journey last year!

As the biggest consumer products company in the world this is no small change.

They also have a plan to gain 1 billion, yes billion new customers in that time – mostly in the third world. Hummm…

Does a strong commitment to energy and waste reduction make them a green company? Are they really green washing? What are the criteria by which we can begin to discern the wannabes from those authentically on the journey? They have mentioned triple bottom line reporting and I can see where being active in the developing world might be counted as part of the triple bottom line. Not mentioned at all was their commitment to reducing the toxins in their products. In developing countries this would be crucial!

I'm very happy and excited that P&G has started on their journey, and given the current level of commitment I expect great things! They are off to a great start and we can only hope that as they get more experience they will address some of these other issues as well.

Their approach is what many of the other major corporations in the world are following: Coke, Unilever, and similar companies are firmly in the first stage of sustainability – learning to reduce their resource use and thereby reducing their ecological footprint. Good on them!

What will the second stage look like for them? What would happen if zero waste became a business strategy? We could start with zero contamination and pollution and move on to making all products with natural (even organic) sources, eliminating all petroleum-based products. That would be a good start and a game changer for the kinds of new products they would be producing. It might also push on their packaging approaches. No waste, maybe that might lead to reclaiming their packaging for reuse and recycling – a key in developing countries where coke bottles can be found in the jungle in the middle of nowhere.

What about the third stage where the Earth is actually better for their presence? Ah! That is fantasyland! How could that be? What amazing changes might that entail and *what* a fantasy that would be! That is where we need to be headed – if we want to be sustainable. That is what must come into being if the businesses that exist now want to be here another 100 years or 10,000 years. Ten thousand years, did I say that? Can you think ahead that far? *That's* being sustainable!

Sustainable Intelligence: Lessons Learned from Earthquakes

The Ecological Thinking inherent in Sustainable Intelligence includes a set of Sustainable Values™, one of which is Dynamic Stability. In ecology it describes the fluid aspect of nature that ebbs and flows by making small incremental changes on a continuous basis. By making small, often unnoticed, changes big shifts are made easily and without pain. Rivers move mountains and forests over take meadows with no one able to tell when it happened or even where the exact boundaries lie.

Deming saw this wisdom in his insistence on continuous improvement. A story is told that the Japanese who had visited American factories after the WWII came again 20 years later. They were astonished, as nothing had changed.

Earthquakes are like that. Much of the movement is incremental, too small to notice. Those small movements over time, place great pressure on those points of contact, until something snaps and the awesome experience of an earthquake takes place.

Think for a moment about the tensions in your own organization. Can you recognize those small movements that are tremors, asking for release? Can you open yourself up to help create the small changes those tremors are asking for?

Think for a moment about our political and economic tremors are we working to make incremental change or are we working to prevent that movement? Are we so frightened by that tension that the mere thought of any movement is terrifying? Are we seeking to return to a time that will never come again instead of moving forward easily, with minimal pain into the future that wants to be born?

It's not that we don't have the strength to make it through huge quakes, we do. An important question has to do with our ability to manage the financial costs on a regular basis. A greater question however, is whether it's ethical to *require* toughing it out just because we are too frightened or so much in denial about those real tremors that we are unwilling to adjust? The human capacity for self-delusion is remarkable. One of the important survival skills we can learn from Mother Nature is the wisdom to welcome incremental change. They speak of learning from history, but too often we insist that this is different and turn a blind eye to the reality right in front of us.

If you understand the lay of the land, then skiing downhill can be fun. If you don't it's dangerous. There are those who only come alive when in danger. There are others who become paralyzed. An artist and a warrior both have in common the ability to see how to get from one point to another. The warrior does so at great cost, to self and others, the artist with great joy, to self and others. Mother Nature cares which response we choose. Do you?

Sustainability and the Survival of the Fittest

I have a presentation I give on Sustainable Intelligence and Business. I speak about how we need to learn to work with nature instead of against her. This message seemed to resonate with 98% of the people there - however there were a few who disagreed.

How can you work with nature when nature can and does work to destroy you? Isn't nature "red in tooth and claw?" Isn't nature nasty and threatening? And isn't nature just a little bit scary? Take the tsunami in Japan, for example.

The answer to all of these concerns of course, is yes - nature can be and is fierce, threatening and scary. There is much more to this however, than just an acknowledgement. The first caveat is that nature is never malicious. By that I mean nature never singles someone out for punishment or pain. Nature works with the whole system in mind and everything she does supports life *for the whole* (it just may not include us).

And that's why working with nature is so important. Many times we go against what she naturally does and then blame her for the consequences. Building in flood plains, is one example. We want to build in a flood plain and we want the government to insure us against the inevitable flooding when we shouldn't build there in the first place. This kind of hubris will be more and more of an issue as our population increases in size. The pressure and greed from a increasing number of people makes it seem like we need to invade and fight against nature to have our way and immediately satisfy our desires, instead of being creative within these natural limits.

I have a friend who regularly sends me tidbits having to do with some very dumb actions on the part of some people called the "Darwin Awards" as the results usually remove them from the gene pool. An example: When his 38 caliber revolver failed to fire at his intended victim during a holdup in Long Beach, California, would-be robber James Elliot did something that can only inspire wonder. He peered down the barrel and tried the trigger again. This time it worked.

Maybe it really is about the Darwin Awards and maybe that's the attitude we should have toward our ignoring Mother Nature...

Can We Be Sustainable Without Reverence?

I've been watching a DVD made to share the wonder that was Thomas Berry. The first Geologian, he spent his life working to bring back or reignite the wonder of nature that lies latent in our hearts.

I fear that our withdrawal from nature into cities of glass and concrete will create a kind of craziness from which our species may not survive. We feel somehow, that cities make us safe, that they protect us from the 'wilds' and the chaos that the wilderness seems to offer. We seem to be more willing to deal with our own 'wildness' than with the perceived 'wildness' of other life.

Of course that path is unsustainable. Our illusions amidst glass and concrete are killing everything they touch, and we are no exception. There will come a tipping point where it will be clear that in order to survive we will need to integrate our own life with that of the other beings on the planet - like Thomas Berry says, the communion of souls. We will survive when we make our cities porous so that life can flow through. We will survive when we make our souls porous, so life can flow through. We will survive when we make our businesses porous - open to nature's wisdom - so life can flow through.

That is what sustainability really means. - a opening up for life to flow through, bringing the diversity, blessings and beauty that makes existence worthwhile.

As I look at the six major threats to our survival and health of the ecosystem (Fracking, GMO, CO_2, willful ecosystem destruction as in mountain top destruction or water system destruction, radiation through waste and malfunction, and population) they are all of human origin and under human control. Five of them are driven by greed. Greed has been masked by cleverness and platitudes about doing good. Its handmaidens are to pretend ignorance and shift responsibility. To act in this way it is necessary to render the 'other' as unimportant, whether the 'other' is another human being, a plant, a mountain, an aquifer or the planet itself. These are the antithesis of reverence.

It is easy to destroy what we don't care for. When we act against our own best interests, no matter how we rationalize it, we can feel as if we do not deserve goodness because we are not good. That can generate an unconscious desire to punish or sabotage ones self. These feelings just perpetuate the destructive cycle and act as an unconscious rationalization for it. How else can you explain the willingness to jeopardize the drinking water for over 15 MILLION people by natural gas mining through fracking?

Why would people even consider such a move? What is going on in their minds?

The truth is that fracking is just another extension of our fear of scarcity and our belief that somehow we are more important than anything else. We will achieve humbleness when we finally realize our interconnections and gain the deep appreciation and gratitude for all the help and support we are offered by the other living things on this wonderful Earth we call home!

Final Thoughts

Can you begin to see how sustainable intelligence is a different way of thinking? Can you see how important it is and how dramatic a shift it makes in our relationship to our world? The key is RELATIONSHIP! This means understanding flow (dynamic stability), reciprocity, limits to growth and caring enough about our future and our home (Earth) to engage in self-discipline. These are the beginning steps to healing our world!

❧

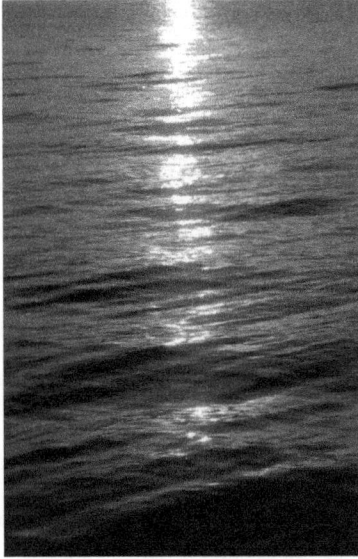

2 New Thoughts on Values – The Sustainable Values Set®

*The major problems of the world are the result of the difference between the way nature works and the way people think". ~**Gregory Bateson**, anthropologist, social scientist, linguist*

The Nature of Value Sets

A Value set is a collection of values that are congruent with each other. Together they form a collective whole, a system. As a system they exhibit all the properties of other living systems. An important part of understanding values sets is to know that they are complete wholes with integral parts. Integral parts cannot be removed from a system or exchanged with another system without compromising the overall integrity of that system.

When we think of ethics and values, we often think of would's and should's, of rights and wrongs, but our tendency to dichotomize betrays the inherent complexity in these concepts.

Our insistence that things should be black and white is confounded by our experience in reality, which is so commonly filled with shades of grey. The complexity of values cannot be understood in a linear way. A value, *by itself,* does not equal or create behavior. Values come in systems, a group of interrelated parts that have a purpose. The systems of values, however, do create behavior.

Our lack of understanding about this has blinded us to both the relationships among certain "sets" of values as well as the purposes they support. We are used to seeing values as independent parts instead of the interdependent components of a system.

This is important because while each value has relevance and meaning by itself, together, as a system, a collection of values has tremendous impact.

Think of the old adage, the sum of the parts is greater than the whole. From a values perspective, that means that those values that form systems pull all the others into action if the core value is used.

There are three such systems and each system has an intent or purpose: protection, effectiveness, or sustainability. The intents can be mutually exclusive which is why mixing the values from each system results in corruption and none of the intents are achieved. (See *Doing What's Right: finding ethics in a sea of values,* by Kathryn Alexander for more on this)

The intent and purpose of the Sustainable Values Set® is nature's intent. These values have been distilled from the work of many people, scientists and philosophers, who have looked at nature to try and discern the *patterns* that underlay her behavior. What does she do that has created the context for the continuing complexity of life? How has she managed to keep our planet healthy and verdant for 3.8 billion years? The Sustainable Values Set® is what I believe is a shared agreement of the values that people can use to mimic her behavior.

The Sustainable Values Set®

1. Commitment

Integrity of the Whole

In living systems integrity is achieved by fit because all systems consist of interdependent and interconnected *parts*. Look at these two lists of characteristics we commonly see in our organizations:

List Number One

Short-term focus
Rigid culture
Leadership from the top

Employee obedience
Dependent on Analysis
Competitive
Win or lose
Individuality prized
Information hoarded

List Number Two
Long-term focus
Flexible culture
Work has meaning
Leadership is facilitative
Cooperation and co-creation
Harmony and trust
Honesty & compassion
Corporate & individual wisdom
Information openly available

Can you see that each 'system' has integrity?
Try changing "Information is horded (secrecy)" to
"Information is openly available" in the first list.
What happens? All of the other characteristics
want to change. With information readily available
then the win or lose disappears as everyone begins
to win. Individuality shifts to 'us', the culture
becomes flexible and so on. By making that one

change, the parts no longer fit and integrity is compromised.

When the purpose is not consciously clear and we try and make changes in organizations, then we can run afoul of the current system integrity. I think this is one of the reasons why we experience resistance to change. People inherently feel that dissonance and if it is not addressed they will work to bring back that feeling of integrity they remember. This pushes the system back into old habits instead of moving forward into new behavior.

In living systems all of the parts are equally important and valid, and all are interdependent and interconnected. An ecosystem is the best example of this. Our cities are also ecosystems, but we do not think of them as such nor manage them as ecosystems. All living systems are wholes that are nested in other systems that are also wholes. Think of families, nested in organizations, nested in cities, nested in states, nested in countries, nested in nature.

Confucius was correct - a healthy society needs healthy families. Because of the interdependence of nesting the health of one part affects all of the other parts. Any action of any part affects the other parts and that affects the whole, but not at the same time, and not in a linear fashion.

Two of the big differences between linear and non-linear cause and effect are time and space. With linear cause and effect the action and response are immediate. In non-linear cause and effect the response may appear in a different place and time.

A new manager is hired in the call center. This person wants his department to be the best, so he doesn't want his people talking to the other departments so any 'dirty laundry' will be kept private. This prevents the call center from sharing with other departments what they are learning from customers. The result is that manufacturing is not told that certain parts are not being produced that customers need for repairs. The change in the system is not seen immediately and the symptom of ineffectiveness (ill health) is not seen where the cause is, but surfaces in another part of the system.

Seeing wholes and understanding patterns are crucial to integrity and ethical action. It is the integrity of the *whole* that is foundation for acting with integrity with the *parts*.

All Actions Create the Conditions that Support Life

Life is not just existence, but the joy in living. It is this joy of life that so refreshes us in nature. This is something that some of the less affluent societies seem to know, why else would countries like Vietnam rank higher on the Happy Planet Index than countries like the United States? This index measures: experienced wellbeing, life expectancy, and ecological footprint.

Actions and thoughts that deny or undermine the joy of living are not life enhancing. For people this often means two things, community and a meaningful life. Struggle that builds capacity is necessary for Life and in many cases gives life meaning. The fascination with safety in developed countries means that most of our basic needs (food, water, home) are met with little effort on our part. The system that makes that possible, however, seems to insulate us from each other and make our work life relatively meaningless.

In response we seek extreme sports where our very life is at risk, or we veg in front of the television in substitution of excitement, or we eat or drink as distractions, seeking ways to spend time. Of this list only one - seeking extreme sports, create the conditions that support Life and that at the very risk of it. Even here the meaning maybe as shallow as winning or as deep as self-competition, which while promoting growth and development, contributes little to the greater whole. It is service to something larger that makes for a deeply meaningful life.

Authenticity is key that brings personal growth and service together. Your body knows when you have acted in a way that supports Life. Those into extreme sports will tell you that the excitement lies on the razors edge of truth, of knowing - in the moment - what is the *right* thing to do. Speed and danger form the context that makes that discipline imperative. The trick is to maintain that same integrity when the pace is slower and the risk less immediate.

Humans are Intrinsic to the Web of Life

In humanity lies the future. As far as we know we are the only species that recognizes the future. We are the only species that can see the future and so we are the only species responsible for bringing the future into existence.

We are the only species, as far as we know, able to see the patterns of the past. That ability to see the pattern of increasing complexity, for instance, allows us something very special - the ability to recognize the intention of creation. The universe can only see and celebrate itself through our species. Through us the universe becomes self-aware. That is a profound gift and a profound responsibility.

We are the only species who can see the entire curve of creation from the past to the present and thus appreciate the increasing complexity of consciousness. We are the only ones capable of seeing wholes and patterns. That gives us the ability to become co-creators with the universe as we work to facilitate the flow.

Acting on what only *we* can see and know is key to our value. As co-creators, then, authenticity is critical as that is the place where we connect to the greater whole and where the voice of the universe is present in us.

Right Relationship

Relationship is an acknowledgement of the value and contribution of the other. Right relationship is acting in that knowledge to preserve and respect that value. In right relationship we see the universe in everything around us and all of our actions strive to preserve our relationship with it in all of its manifestations.

2. Continuity

Precautionary Principle

Nothing is more important than the future of Life, so all actions are mitigated to ensure both continuation of Life, the health of life, the joy of Life and the relationships needed to sustain that life.

Attention is paid to the implications and consequences of all decisions. When there is doubt about the impact on Life or the decision

appears damaging, no action is taken. The tension
between desire and possible consequences is used
to create a new and Life enhancing solution.
Because future consequences are more important
than immediate need, this tension becomes a
source of creativity, making the results worth the
patience.

This is the discipline that will make the
process of creativity conscious and consistent
with our intent of supporting Life. This discipline
will help ensure the integrity of our actions over
time. The Precautionary Principle is the path to
integrity and is what connects our present with
our future.

Sometimes people misunderstand the
Precautionary Principle to mean 'no' when what it
really means is 'wait and work until it fits'. This is
a vastly different undertaking than stopping or
quitting altogether. It asks us to listen to nature
and intertwine our desires with hers. Most often it
is not the 'what' but the 'how' that gets us into
trouble.

Interdependency

Interdependency suggests that we acknowledge our debt and responsibility to other life forms. Nothing exists on its own without the contribution and support of something else. All of us rely on others, even if they are far removed in time and space. Native peoples understand this to mean that we owe a debt to our ancestors. We are the ancestors of the future. Nothing exists independently.

To remove any part of this chain of Life is to put the entire chain at risk. Nature thinks in systems and not in things. All things are interconnected and as such each entity impacts everything else, but that impact is in a non-linear cause and effect manner.

We can speculate that we are most dependent upon what there is the most of: soil, air, water and microbes. All of these we have treated with disrespect and are in danger of losing. Sometimes I think God must have a sense of humor and just role in the isles over what we doing. How else can we look at the fact that we are destroying our life and calling it progress? Not only that we seem willing to work harder and pay more for the privilege of doing so! *That* is funny!

It may be apparent that we interdependent, but we don't seen to respect that dependency. In fact we seem to resist it and act as though being dependent makes us weak. We forget that if we are strong and help others then we are dependent upon them to accept our help. Being *inter*dependent is not quite the same as being dependent, but you can be one without the other.

Optimization

The goal is to make the *whole* healthy and successful – to be the best it can be. We tend to maximize parts and sacrifice the health of the whole, in doing so. We often don't see connections, and even when we do we dismiss them as unimportant or assume they will rebuild themselves 'like magic.'

From nature's perspective the parts are important, but only in so far as they contribute to the whole. This may sound harsh, but good marriages *are* good because both parties focus on the health of the relationship (how they *fit* with each other) instead of their own needs. By optimizing the whole (in this case the relationship) everyone is happy.

The same is true for each level of system: family, organization, city, state, country, planet. Nature's structure for this is the ecosystem, which is really a system of nested wholes. Optimization is the capacity of seeing that all of the parts of a system work well together. In the marriage example, *both* parties need to be happy and each needs to be sensitive to the other, making sure that their needs are met, all the while monitoring their own state, making sure both (themselves and their partner) are happy. Too often we focus on our own happiness - to the detriment of others.

In organizations the various departments all need to be conscious of how they work with each other - how they *fit* together. This has been called the 'white space' in the organization. It is where work is handed off between departments. There are organizations (manufacturing runs into this) where a part will have a different name/number in each department. In such situations there is no *fit* as things have to be created anew in each area. Flow, in many companies, can be a better indicator of organizational health than individual departmental goal achievement. In fact, unless departmental goals are established coherently, across the organization, they can actually *prevent fit.*

Understanding that all things have a season we can learn to work with the natural cycles of growth, allowing for fallow times. Working within natural rhythms maintains the health of the whole. There *are* times where the focus needs to be on one aspect or part of a system, but that focus has to be allowed to shift as other needs present themselves. The key is not losing sight of what health looks like for the *entire* system.

Because symptoms in systems show up in a non-linear manner, finding the root cause of the problem can be hard. It is wise to look at the impact on the system of the symptom and seek solutions where that impact is created - no matter where that symptom occurs, asking 'why' from three to five times will get to the root cause of the issue.

This is a lot easier than it sounds. My favorite example comes from the Ritz-Carlton hotel in San Francisco.

Ritz-Carlton prides itself on customer service. When you stay there everyone knows

WHAT'S IT MEAN – SHIFTING TO GREEN?

your name and your personal preferences – at any hotel in the world. A manager in the San Francisco hotel decided to offer a $125 refund if room service wasn't satisfactory. All of a sudden he began to notice that they were paying out a *lot* of $125 refunds because the food was arriving cold.

So the presenting problem was that the food was arriving cold. The servers were taking elevators up to the rooms and they had to wait for elevators. Now take a minute and come with a solution or two to this issue, in your own mind.

The first question to ask is why are they waiting for elevators? They looked into that and found that the maids were using the elevators when they cleaned rooms. Now take a minute and rethink your previous solution. Have any new ideas?

Then they ask why the maids were using the elevators. The maids were using the elevators because there were not enough towels. SO, the food was cold because there were not enough towels. They didn't need to add elevators, or invest in hot boxes, or dedicate an elevator or any of the other creative solutions you might have come up with *that would have eliminated the problem, but NOT solved it.* They really needed to buy more towels. In doing so they solved the *root cause* of the cold food and solved several other problems at the same time. This is a perfect example of non-linear cause and effect! Solving the *root cause* optimizes the entire system.

3. Resilience

Self-Organization

Self-Organization is the ability for people to take action in a way that enhances their comfort, effectiveness, and sustainability by accessing all the information they need from their environment. Acting this way also supports and enhances the ability of others to do the same.

Patterns of behavior arise that achieve coherence through the sharing of information. Directive leadership is not necessary and gets in the way. A good example of this is the flight of a flock of birds. How would you like your company to act like this? The birds only pay attention to the birds on each side and they respond to any slight changes.

In most companies information is hidden on a 'needs to know' basis. But who determines the need to know and by the time permission is gained things have changed. There are tools to help remember who to connect with after meetings, and ways to designing meetings so additional connections are moot. Much of the frustration about not being included in the decision is not intentional. People don't know who needs to know and they forget in the rush to get things done. It is also not convenient as now we often work in teams that are not co-located.

Mastering this capability is the number one key to building a responsive company. It is not enough to *know* about something – people also have to feel free/empowered to use the information. Notice in the video that the birds did not always go the same way, but the form stayed connected. It takes constant sharing, clarity about the shared vision, the freedom to experiment, the maturity to not blame, and joy in being responsible for self-organization to work. Self-organized cultures are dynamic and robust, innovative and fun to work in!

Diversity

Diversity expresses the richness of life. In nature it is how life replenishes itself and guarantees its evolutionary capacity and sustainability.

For individuals, diversity allows for resilience, increased capacity and capability, exceptional creativity and expanded consciousness. The more you know, the more interests you have the more insight you can bring to bear on issues you face.

For companies the same is true. A divergence of opinions is necessary to find healthy solutions. Each point of view holds some truth, so by working to address and include that truth you also ensure a solution that will last have fewer unexpected consequences.

In living systems there is always more than one solution. Taking the time and having the resources to provide more than three options expands your possibilities in major ways. What is obvious to one person/one part of the system is unseen by another. Instead of arguing for *your* truth, seeing the truth – taking time to *find* the truth in what others are saying, is central to using diversity well.

Our brains naturally get caught in polarization when there are only two options. Not only that we feel we *must* choose one, even if it isn't quite right. With at least three choices, real concerns can come out as there is space to decide and less of a feeling of compulsion. Try it when you are trying to make small decisions, like where to go to eat or for a movie. Present three options and see if you don't arrive at a decision quicker.

Reciprocity

Reciprocity is the expression of mutual respect for the value others bring through the open receipt of their gifts. The acknowledgement of value through the giving and receiving flow cements both culture and community. It is exchange without debt.

What is important about reciprocity is that it is about *flow*. It is circular and requires all participants to engage. It is not giving. Giving is a one way street and is often used; for selfish reasons, to play one upmanship, to exert power over, to enmesh in debt, and to salve consciences instead of really dealing with things. In short giving is often about manipulation.

The corollary of giving this way is taking. Taking is also manipulative and often undermines self-esteem. It is a one-down position, or it is deceptive and seen as a sort of corrupted one upmanship. In this dance both parties are colluding to side step the real issue in order to get something for themselves.

Taking seems to cover up the dependence that is at the core of the interdependence that reciprocity is an expression of. Reciprocity is *how* interdependence is made manifest. Taking creates the illusion of control and demeans the real value of the exchange.

Reciprocity is about honoring the urge to give and the willing receipt by the other. It is a valued exchange on both sides and the values lies in the act, more than what is exchanged. Reciprocity is delicate and often spontaneous – a natural outpouring from the heart. It is in the *receiving* that the value is established and honored. Reciprocity is an expression of both gratitude and appreciation.

Reciprocity is what greases the wheel of community by creating flow. It is a mechanism for expressing and validating value for relationship. Reciprocity is an exchange between equals in recognition of the importance of the relationship and in gratitude for it.

Reciprocity is a lesson I learned as I addressed my stage 3b liver cancer. I discovered it was a gift to receive from those who wanted to give and that the desire to give, to help, was not about *me*, but simply about the fact that I was another/fellow human being. This was a very humbling experience and a lesson I am very grateful to have been given!

Dynamic Stability

This is the ability of living systems to move incrementally in concert with its changing environment in such a way that while the change can be significant the discomfort is minimal or almost non-existent and the new stable state is achieved while maintaining the integrity of the whole system.

We see this in rivers and in how our own bodies grow. Changes happen subtly but consistently so that, over time, major change is accomplished, but the disruption has been minimal or non-existent.

The Total Quality movement saw continuous change as the way to achieve major shifts in companies without causing major disruptions, fear or risk. Seemingly minor changes accumulate and create dramatic change, in the long run.

Dynamic Stability exists when the tension between continuity and change is maintained and neither is acceded to. Changes are made that improve the entire system while causing the least discomfort. This approach costs less, has less risk, less resistance and achieves the greatest benefit, over time.

Empowerment

Authentic actions spring from the recognition of significant value in self and others so that it becomes immoral to withhold that value or prevent its expression. It is power with. Empowerment is about enabling the innate talents and capabilities to flower and bloom. It is seeing in others what others might not see in themselves.

Power is an interesting thing. Usually, when we seek push – *making* others do what we want. We feel we are really doing the work and we want the rewards and we fear the consequences if we fail. That dynamic, because it is false, creates underlying layers of helplessness (we really can't control others or circumstances) and fear (of not really being in control and feeling out of control).

We see others as a means to our own ends as so at the affect of what they do or don't do, not a very 'powerful' place to be. This leads to anger, anxiety and frustration as 'they' don't seem to care, 'they' don't seem to understand, and 'they' do the most unexpected and off purpose (ours) things that *we* have to deal with, change, or clean up. Geesh!

Empowerment is really about utilizing the power that resides in the system – the power that others innately have. When the focus is on what *we* can accomplish then we often actively discourage others – in effect disempowering them. This is one of the major leadership skills that effective leaders learn – how to evoke the best from others.

People are much more easily discouraged than encouraged. We have been habituated to discouragement from birth as we strove to please parents and teachers who were better at discouraging than encouraging.

Here's a graphic, The Power Continuum I designed to help people see what power is all about, where it really resides and how to use it effectively.

The "Power Fields" Continuum

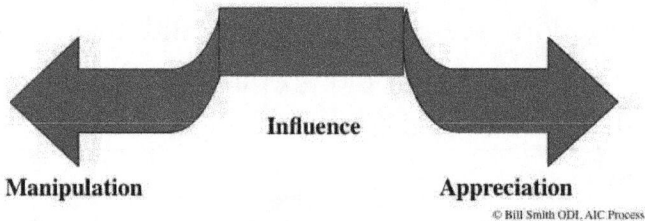

Influence

Manipulation   Appreciation

© Bill Smith ODI, AIC Process

Most ways power is used is a form of manipulation. This happens in two ways; through rewards and bribes and by punishment. We offer bonuses and other incentives to those who perform as we ask. These tend to stimulate short-term behavior spurts and work best when tied to very specific goals and objectives. Incentives can also generate questionable and problematic behavior as people game the systems to obtain rewards. One of the major unintended consequences of this approach is unethical and illegal behavior.

Punishment can be overt or tacit, it can be as simple as a personal expression of disfavor to the loss of a job. Punishment and the threat or potential for punishment is a major factor in discouraging others to contribute. For many the risk factor is just too great, so contributions are withheld in self-protection.

The effectiveness of manipulation stems from the fact that it is immediate. The person in control has the ability to directly impact those being controlled – for good or ill – in real time. This is why it is effective, but it is also an inherent weakness. People work to game the system or work around constraints so over time this form of power decreases or it has to be consistently reapplied. The fear of loss reduces creativity and curtails innovation as does the focus on a single individuals small groups vision. Trying to read the mind of those in control is a recipe for confusion, in the long run.

Often the 'vision' the leader is holding is one that is self-serving, gaining wealth, status or personal control over something or other people. Because the real rewards are not really shared, the coercion of force (punishment) or the apparent sharing through limited rewards is necessary to engage others.

The middle of the Continuum sees power as Influence instead of Manipulation. Influence can be fear or appreciation based, but it expands the range and timeframe of effectiveness. Trying to emulate someone reduces the fear (of being wrong, of disappointing, of making someone else angry) and so increases the willingness to take risks and be innovative.

It is easy to understand how wanting to be like someone leads to behavior that is more in line with the desires of the leader than fearing what would happen to you if the leader disapproved. When the vision is held by someone else there is always some fear present, as only the holder of the vision really understands it. At the manipulative end of the Continuum the leader is trying to get others to live their vision, when influence takes over there is a genuine attempt by the followers to act *as though the vision is theirs.* The leaders vision becomes something to be desired and something that can be engaged with *for its own sake.* This expansion increases the power by building momentum.

When a leader with a powerful vision has become influential that influence no longer requires the leaders presence to be effective. The leader no longer has to be in a position of having to directly and immediately reward or punish to encourage behavior. At this stage the followers are actively searching for behavior that they feel the leader would approve of and desire instead of only doing as they are told.

Because the focus is still on the leader and the leaders vision there are inherent limits to this form of power, just as there are with manipulation. Trying to please others is inherently scary. The nuances are difficult to discern and there may be aspects that are either confusing or uncomfortable or both. This is especially true when the vision holds others as being 'less than' or when it actively causes pain and suffering to others. There is a very fine line between 'us' and 'them,' which is one reason why fear is such a limiting factor.

The key to effective, long-term power seems to be who holds the vision. The

Appreciative kind of power gets its energy from the *shared* vision. When the vision lives in the hearts and minds of everyone who is implementing it, then the fear disappears and each person is able to evaluate and strengthen the contributions of others. When you *know* that others are working for the same ends, then it is easy to *appreciate* what they are doing and how they are doing it. I mentioned earlier the 'us/them' issue and that is razor's edge. It is easy to make a 'them' out of those who don't share the vision. It is *very* easy when the vision itself is exclusive instead of being inclusive, and *that* is the razor's edge. The Klu Klux Clan is a good example. Their 'vision' is exclusive and is deliberately creating an 'us/them' dichotomy. It is fear based, not love and respect based. It is here that the two core values: maintaining the integrity of the whole, and creating the conditions that support Life come into play in evaluating a vision. If a vision doesn't express these two fundamental aspects of nature; maintaining the integrity of the whole and creating conditions to support Life, then it is *not* Life enhancing and thus not sustainable.

From a leadership perspective, the sharing of the vision and the willingness to grow it with input so it lives with the experience of those doing the implementation is crucial. When people talk about juicy visions and the ability of a vision to facilitate decision-making, this is what they mean. A truly shared vision taps into the highest and best values the implementers hold, so as they work to make the vision real the *implementers* become better people – they become the people they envision themselves to be, that they wish and want to be. *That* is why it is shared!

A shared vision becomes a yardstick by which all actions are measured. This requires a willingness to share mistakes, learning experiences, and crushing blows openly so everyone learns and the understanding of what actions actually achieve the goal can get refined. This takes strong and committed leadership! No one is immune from mistakes, so here is where walking the talk defines the reality and authenticity show up, without them the vision is just window dressing and this is something that can't be hidden or manufactured. Authentic behavior requires letting go of the ego, without that achieving Appreciative power is impossible. Empowering others is about releasing the power inherent in others in pursuit of the *shared* vision.

4. Fertility/Innovation

I deliberately choose the word *fertility* to both expand our understanding of innovation and how it comes about, but also to bring in a more feminine point of view. I added *innovation* for those uncomfortable with this change. We speak of a *fertile imagination* as being indicative of creativity. It is my belief that thinking about creating *fertile* situations – situations pregnant with possibility is one step in allowing emergence to take place. Peggy Holman, in her book *Engaging Emergence* showcases many ways to do this. The values in this section are also ways to foster the conditions that create a fertile ground for continuous innovation and creativity, something for which nature is renown!

As we watch the collapse of so many systems upon which we've come to depend, the need for thinking differently has never been greater. Margaret Wheatley and the Berkana Institute have been instrumental in helping to change our thinking as well as how we work together. Her article on the lifecycle of emergence is well worth noting!

Co-Creation

This is an expression of the recognition of the right of all life to self-fulfillment and self-actualization and co-creating is how that right is mutually reinforced. Co-creation is not collaboration. People collaborate when they join forces to accomplish something. In collaboration it is usually easy to distinguish who did what and in fact the work is often parceled out that way.

In co-creation it is not possible to tell who did what. The finished product is a whole, complete unto itself and indivisible into separate parts. All who participated are clear that the others were needed and that nothing would have happened if any one of the participants had not been there. The skills and unique contributions of each party were necessary for the whole to be accomplished.

Co-creation requires passion and commitment, but no ego. It happens when the task at hand becomes bigger than any of the creators. It is evidence of a dedication to something bigger than the individuals taking part in the actuation of the dream or vision. Co-creation generates a joy and excitement all of its own and that experience becomes the reward for participating. The journey is more interesting and exciting than the arrival or accomplishment of the task. When the task is done the participants think, "We did it!" not "I did it."

Co-creation leads to deep trust and appreciation of the other participants. The unique contribution of each individual is recognized and valued and the solidarity built generates a lasting trust. This can be a heady atmosphere and a very cherished experience. Working this way shows what we are capable of and being valued can be a life-changing experience.

Ecologies

Ecological thinking is thinking as an expression of the community of interdependence, ensuring abundance, sufficiency and mutual health for all participants. Ecologies are networks or interconnections of individuals and groups who are all working to bring forth life and health as they co-create the world anew. Ecologies are communities of living beings who need each other to ensure a mutually healthy existence. All parts of the ecology are alive and relevant and contributing and receiving so that individual needs are met as well as the needs of the whole. They are wholes and when broken apart they suffer.

Ecologies are essential to the elimination of waste. As we have begun to apply this concept to business, the idea of industrial ecology was born.

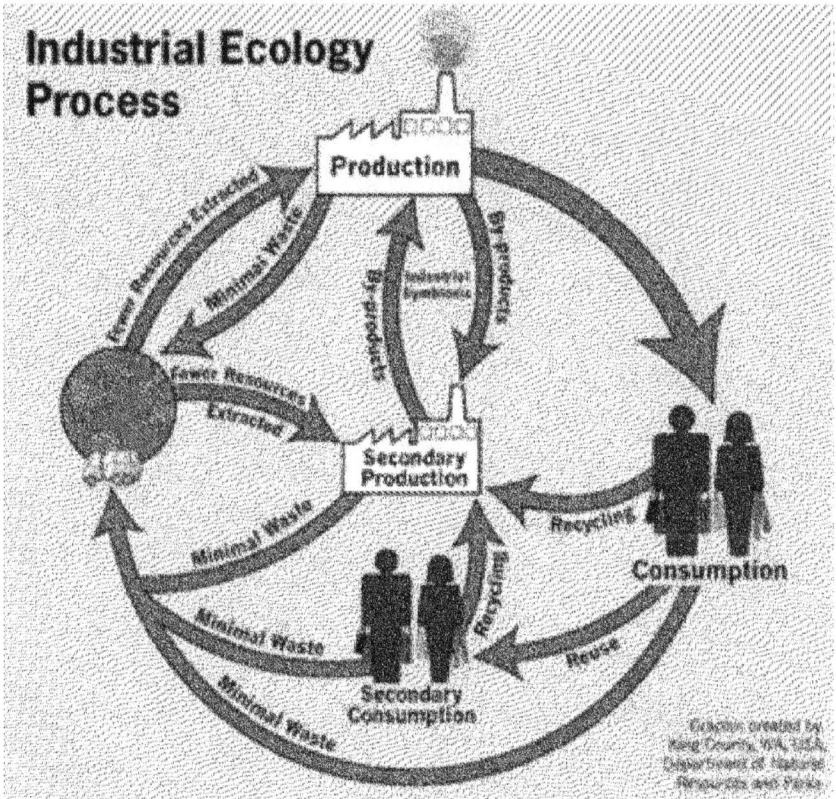

This takes planning and is difficult to do when you need to have many different types of businesses located close enough that they can use each other's waste. There are a few examples, the

<u>City of Kalundborg, Denmark</u> is one, but the difficulty of getting the right companies together at the right time and in the right place have severely limited this experiment.

What business has to learn is that they already *are* part of an ecology. The clearest example of this is wages. When people are paid enough that they can not only meet basic needs but have a surplus, then they buy. When companies like McDonald's and Walmart are subsidized by taxpayers through government programs like Medicaid and Food Stamps, then they are diminishing the health of the local/national ecology. They are requiring other members of the ecosystem to do what they should be doing, thus limiting the health and growth that is possible. Even small stores are caught in this misconception when they only pay minimum wage. When employees are at survival, even though they are working, then they are not focused on business needs, but personal needs and they can't contribute to the health and growth of the economic ecology either. Ecologies are about *all* of us, it is an all or nothing proposition. That they don't collapse immediately only feeds the illusion that others don't matter.

Zero Waste

In nature nothing is created that can't be eaten and everything that can be eaten is. Nothing is withheld from taking its place as nourishment for someone else; this means there is no waste in nature.

In contrast, Western humans believe that things can be 'thrown away' and that their bodies are too precious to decompose. In nomadic times our movement allowed nature to reclaim and recycle our waste. As we began staying in one place for longer and longer times, waste became an issue as did the environmental destruction necessary to build homes and keep warm.

Various societies have addressed these issues in various ways, with varying measures of success. The mountain communities of Peru, Machu Picchu etc. were exceptionally clever in how they did this. The terracing and aqueducts required tremendous planning and sophisticated engineering to make life both livable and healthy. Because mountain environments are sparse and demanding, refuse could not be allowed to accumulate and had to be dealt with. It is not easy planning for 1000 people, even for a short time.

Previous civilizations, however, have not had to deal with the tremendous amount of man-made materials. We make food out of petroleum, which our bodies have never before ingested, so we have no evolutionary adaption mechanisms in place to digest it well. There are bacteria that eat petroleum, and they are useful in some situations. What are we thinking when we put antifreeze in baked goods?

The damage done by drugs that make it through the water 'purification' process as shellfish and who knows what else, mutate when ingesting them, is only barely known and hard to track. The 'away' that flushing down the toilet presents, is an illusion.

In nature multiple uses at multiple levels constitutes a system that reuses every resource many times over. This compares to our 'throw away' society where one use is deemed sufficient. There is always excess; in contrast we want ALL the fish in the ocean and we kill many species we don't want just to ensure that get as much as we can of the species we do want. This practice generates waste upon waste, and makes it difficult for a species to recover, since we leave so few. We also take the biggest, oldest and most experienced, leaving behind the least likely to survive. The excess in nature we equate with sloppiness in human terms, not seeing the benefit of that 'sloppiness' to other life forms.

Deeply understanding waste - what is waste and what is not; what can be reused and recycled and what cannot; and making sure that everything finds its right place of use is *not* easy! Seeking to do so is *the* major driver of substantial change in any business or personal life. The idea of waste is so corrupted and entangled with greed and pride that freeing those misconceptions opens up whole new vistas of possibility. It is one of the best drivers of change!

Curiosity & Experimentation

Learning is at the heart of what it means to be alive and central to what it means to be human. Emergence is an active part of evolution and evolution is a natural consequence of learning. The conditions for emergence have to be cultivated and allowed as they can't be forced or 'created.' This is another way of saying that ambiguity and disorder must become more valued than control as they are a necessary part of the context for emergence. This is a tall order for a species that prides itself on what it can achieve and on what it has accomplished. There is a certain humility necessary in learning, that can be hard for ego driven people to accede to.

Playfulness is the attitude that lets curiosity become a friend. Experimentation is the process that lets curiosity discover truth and innovation, so mistakes become the measure of commitment and courage. Each of these speak to cultures that hold the value of learning above image by supporting a willingness to be humble and awed instead of proud.

The key to learning is making mistakes. For most people and most organization cultures mistakes are events that produce shame, fear, and guilt and are things to be covered up and hidden. Mistakes prod people into lying, cheating and covering things up. None of these behaviors produce learning. When mistakes are held against the people involved or when negative or unexpected results impact self-esteem, then there is no learning from the experience – for those involved or others. This means that the same mistake can happen again and again. A costly situation for both the organization and the people involved. Making mistakes *shared learning* experiences is the task of leadership.

There are industries (medicine, construction, and law, for instance) where the ability to learn from experience would make a huge difference. These industries shy away from doing recaps or sharing mistakes out of fear of law suites. This is one indication of the tremendous negative impact the *system* has on learning. One that is costly both in financial terms and in terms of human suffering. There **have been some steps**, particularly in medicine, to protect participants so that learning can be shared without repercussions and the results are encouraging.

Learning is an emotional experience so being open to <u>both the emotional highs and the lows of</u> succeeding and failing ensures that energy is available to get it right. If you deny the lows then the highs are also out of reach.

These are the values that nature uses to ensure the increase in complexity and consciousness that has been the path of Life on Earth for the past 3.8 billion years.

༄

Final Thoughts

Systems thinking to difficult if you are used to thinking about things one step at a time, but the lack of systems thinking is a the root of so many of your current issues (most of which are systemic) that *not* learning how to think in wholes is…unthinkable.

The hidden dynamics in our belief and values systems are only visible when we take a systems perspective. Doing so can remove the tendency to 'blame' others, circumstances, or even our selves for the unintended consequences that we become faced with at times.

The lists of values in each value system (an there is one more system that is talked about in more depth in *What's It Mean – Shifting To Green?*) can be used almost like a checklist when making decisions to ensure that implications and consequences are being thought about.

૭

3 Sustainable Ethics

We are what we pretend to be, so we must be careful about what we pretend to be. ~**Kurt Vonnegut**

A Complicated Morality

Sustainable ethics are complicated and extremely simple at the same time. In these three pieces the *application* of an ethic that is both systemic and holistic brings attention to the tremendous impact nature's values can have on human experience. We have gotten into this situation slowly, but we need to extradite ourselves quickly. In the end, this entire book is about applying sustainable values to our personal and business lives. Here I am only scratching the surface.

The Economics of Waste Versus Ecologies

In the current economic system, using a "parts and pieces" point of view, there is never enough, true costs are 'externalized,' and the flow of wealth is uni-directional. In an economy of ecologies with its attention on wholes, there is always enough, all 'costs' are balanced, and wealth is distributed throughout the system. This is not airy-fairy new age thinking – this is ecological thinking and sustainable intelligence.

By taking a human-centric viewpoint, we have extracted ourselves from the integrated system that supports Life on this planet and overlaid it with a system of our own construction that only took into consideration those aspects that we felt were important. That left everything else a 'mystery' and one that we interpreted as dangerous because it seemed to undo everything we created. Instead of questioning our own behavior, we decided to 'master' that mystery – to control and conquer it.

This attitude has often been credited to Francis Bacon. To quote from Carolyn Merchant's, Philosophy of Francis Bacon, in her work, "The Violence of Impediments" Francis Bacon and the Origins of Experimentation:

> One of Bacon's earliest (though posthumously published) works, "The Masculine Birth of Time" (written in 1602–1603), already contained the subtitle that would characterize his mature program of the 1620s: "The Great Instauration of the Dominion of Man over the Universe." Out of this early interest in the mechanical and practical arts, Bacon began to develop an experimental method

by which nature could be studied and
altered by "art and the hand of man" in
the vast project of extending "the power
and dominion of the human race itself over
the universe."

This approach to nature has infiltrated our thinking in so many ways that it has become an unconscious context for all of our decisions about how we should live on this planet. It is also the point of view that has prevented us from learning *from* nature and instead pushed us to learn *about* nature. The consequence of this is that if we don't have an interest in natural things, we don't see any relevance of the natural world in what we want to do. Wisdom and elegance inherent in natural law is invisible to us.

The problem of course, is that our approach is not working. It has offered considerable benefits for the past 400 years, but that is a drop in the bucket to the 5 million years we have been on the planet. It is also apparent that we cannot continue the same behavior for another 400 years.

By 'externalizing' costs, our current economic system provides a false picture of both cost and profit. Our ability to design a one-way flow of wealth has been at the heart of our beliefs about scarcity and much of the human misery we have inflicted upon each other for centuries. Mother Nature has never inflicted the pain and suffering on us which we have managed to inflict upon ourselves *and then, we justify it,* so we do not even question our actions.

The recent economic crisis exposed the weaknesses and human fallibilities that exist in the current system. By rethinking just two aspects - externalization and uni-directional flow - we can expose the illusion that there is not 'enough.' The application of nature's laws and processes to economic concerns will open up new ways of thinking that will ensure prosperity for everyone. Waste is the enemy of wealth.

Green Business and the Issue of Compliance

I'm starting to see the same confusion in sustainability and the green movement that I see in ethics. In the search for standards and direction, green businesses are looking for, and in some cases asking for, regulation. As government

regulations get created, danger lies in the
confusion that compliance means sustainability,
just like not breaking the law means being ethical.
Neither is true.

Quite apart from the fact both parties with
an agenda to advance can create standards and
laws, both miss the point. Each try to predict the
future by looking in the rearview mirror, and
because of that they address symptoms, not the
root cause of the problem.

I love this idea, from *The Natural Step for
Business: Wealth, Ecology and the Evolutionary
Corporation* by Brian Nattrass & Mary Altomare –
"a company can sail along the familiar coastline of
regulatory compliance and incremental
improvement based on present conditions
extrapolated into a predictable future, but it may
be of little use in the stormy waters of the global
economy and increasing, changing and uncertain
ecological pressures."

There is no vision in sustainability
compliance, so there exists no attempt to build
now to prevent further problems. Without a
vision that addresses the constantly evolving
understanding of what constitutes a healthy

ecosystem, all our actions will become directed at catching up. This is the same reason you can't legislate morality.

The actions that constitute healthy Life-enhancing relationships are made in the moment and are always moral. They can't be regulated, but must be evoked from the caring, respect and authentic responses that are at the heart of any dynamic and meaningful relationship.

The intent and desire for a meaningful relationship come first, then the openness to learning and experimentation, coupled with dialogue and continuous feedback and a fierce commitment to self-understanding.

Humanity is the only species that is a master of self-delusion. Our ability to rationalize may be one of our major self-defining and unsustainable skills. We need to hold the relationship more important than our egos or we will perish in a whirlpool of rationalization and denial.

The Value of Sustainable Values

Most of the decisions we make have a foundational intent. We want to be safe, we want to do a good job, or we want to be sustainable. We haven't made that last choice often because it gets pre-empted by the other two. As we enter an era of uncertainty, the first choice is likely to get more traction, but it will undercut our ability to successfully make the needed transition.

We are facing the unique test of expanding our understanding of 'us,' enabling the entire planet to move forward together, or devolving back into 'every person for himself' ensuring none of us will move forward.

A new and strong understanding of the values that support a sustainable approach - one that ensures the whole planet is considered - will create a robust decision-making context to get us where we want to go, and do it in a manner different from the way of working that got us into this crisis.

Our tendency to see parts and not wholes, makes it difficult to see how to make decisions with the whole (all life) in mind. By tying a clear value system to the same values that operate in nature, we can align our actions *with* those of nature, working with her instead of against her.

The Sustainable Values Set® is just such a tool. The Sustainable Values Set® is part of the Strategic Values Set™ and consists of about 15 values that work together to ensure robust and life enhancing decisions. In working with the Strategic Values Set™, it is possible to see how the values inherent in the other two foundational intents can either get in the way, or support our quest for sustainability.

I applaud our move to use less energy and reduce carbon. We will not survive without doing so. However, by using cost reduction as the prime motivator, we are actually 'doing business as usual' by not shifting or clarifying our intentions. This means that in the long run, we will continue to make decisions that are not aligned with the need to bring our actions back into alignment with nature. This will undermine our success in achieving a sustainable lifestyle.

Because the path forward is so ambiguous and we are creating it as we go, it is remarkably easy to lose our way. Even in the past, maintaining alignment has been difficult and confusing. Going forward it will be even more so as we struggle to create new life-supporting habits.

Our value systems are the trail markers that tell us in which direction we are headed. They tell us if we are more focused on our individual survival, making our task or project successful or if we are working with a deep understanding of the impacts of our actions on other life. If we can't make the shift from me to us, I do not see how we can effectively get through this crisis.

Final Thoughts

Values create the *how* of our behavior. They manage the boundaries of what we can and cannot do. Clarity here is essential to achieve true integrity and coherence over the long-term. Being clear on the values you live buy makes it *much* easier to be accountable and comfortable in your integrity. Rarely do people really think through their values. When I do values clarification work I find that people often conflate the unimportant with the important and what they know others wish with what they authentically desire. Values can be tricky and when we are unclear they are even more so.

The Sustainable Values Set® can be found in Chapter 2.

4 Improving Business

*If you have a dysfunctional institution,
don't try to change it. Rather, determine
what that institution was supposed to
deliver and design a better system to
actually deliver that purpose or service. If
you have done the thing correctly, then
people will come to you for that. The old
institution will eventually wither and die.*
~Bill Mollison, *founder of
Permaculture*

Working *On* the Business, Not Just In It

There are some specific actions that any business leader can take to jump start improving any business. That these approaches are rarely taken is both a factor of not knowing how and of being consumed by the everyday push of business. In many respects, the absence is an indication of the lack of maturity of the business, for mature companies do not require continuous push. The major topics covered in this book - systems thinking, sustainability, and ethics bring benefits to all businesses of any size. One of the major lessons is that to be different you have to act differently, and these pieces help clarify that distinction.

Thinking Strategically

Most small business owners are consumed with the day-to-day details, hoping that sales keep coming. The focus is short term, in the belief that if you take care of today, then tomorrow will be OK.

This works for the most part, for very small companies. These kinds of businesses are really jobs, with the owner being among those employed. The dream and goal is to make ends meet, pay the bills and get along.

However, if your business is a bit bigger, if you are hoping to sell it or if your business just happens to be something you really care about, then you need to think differently.

I say need to think differently, because it is very easy to get caught up in the day-to-day issues and in doing so, you are not managing the business the business is managing you. That is a dangerous state of affairs.

Stages of Development

Businesses have different needs at different sizes. Early on cash flow, actually performing the work and seeking sales are consuming issues. Everyone is excited. You, the leaders walk on water and half the fun for everyone involved is the chance to wear different hats.

Once the market has accepted your offering and you have less than 20 employees, communication becomes a big issue. Capital and hiring begin to demand attention. Survival isn't the issue, consistency is. Here, the wise leader is one who begins to think about delegation and culture. The leader needs to make these ideas solid and conscious or pay the piper later.

With over twenty employees the structure and design of the company, including culture become painful if they were not addressed when things were simpler. Values play a stronger role, as the culture and communication at the core of the company become major forces in aligning and integrating new folks.

Strategy and Resilience

In all of these stages and the ones to follow, vision, values and strategic direction act as the glue and compass, to keep everyone going in the same direction. When is the best time to begin to think strategically? In the beginning! A good strategy is resilient and flexible. It is not about casting things in stone, it is about having a clear sense of direction so decisions are easier and coherent, then you won't find yourself backtracking.

There are many ways to Philadelphia - if one way is blocked, has a problem or time gets short you can easily choose another, but you will only get to Philadelphia if you know that's where you are going. Flexibility comes with a clear direction. Making changes without knowing where you are going is not being flexible - it is being wishy-washy and/or confused - a very different thing.

If sustainability is a key value then using a tool like the Sustainable Values Set can help keep both alignment and coherence in all of your decision-making. Sustainability offers clarity of vision that does the same thing making alignment easy.

Things to Remember

Think strategically, early and often. Understand what stage of development you are in and act accordingly.

If you don't know where you are going, any road will get you there.

Business Plan - Strategic Planning: What's the Difference?

It pains me that there is confusion about the difference between a business plan and strategic planning, but there is. They are complementary, but serve different purposes and should be created in different ways and for different reasons.

Business Plan

There are two purposes for a good business plan. The first is to make sure that the business needs have been thoroughly thought through. I find that doing this once a year you can almost forget it and that, when you check in next year you will be surprised how much you have accomplished. It is sort of a road map of what you want to accomplish with thoughts and ideas about how that might happen.

I find most entrepreneurs and small business owners may not know certain aspects of the business needs – like, how to market nationally, yet there might hesitation about hiring an expert. Planning often seems like 'busy work' and not germane to day-to-day business needs, so it gets put off. If the business is small, making a plan seems like work and is not inspiring or alternatively the owner and a few folks talk about several pressing areas, which makes everyone feel they know enough so writing down a plan seems superfluous.

The second reason for a business plan, and most popular, is for investors. Here you are making a case for the value and projected financial outcome based on their investment dollars by showing them how you intend to spend the money and achieve the expected results.

There is the possibility that you can hire someone to write the plan for you. This gets it done and can teach the business owner a lot, but there can be a disconnect between the written desire, the stated direction, and the business owner, which makes it hard to steer in that direction in the everyday press of business.

Strategic Planning

Gathering a few top people and kicking around ideas about where the company should go in the next few years do traditional strategic planning. Ideas and directions are presented, costs, resources and barriers are discussed and tactics to take the company in that new direction are formulated. Then everyone goes back to their areas and tells everyone what's going to happen.

Common problems are while the plan is real; there is rarely any implementation. The other common issue is getting everyone on the same page, as there can be hidden agendas that color the plan to suit specific needs, which may not serve the entire business. Both of these issues make implementation moot.

Collaborative Strategic Planning

Planning collaboratively allows everyone in the company to participate *and* allows for the wisdom of all stakeholders to contribute. By adding new input, out-of-the-box thinking can occur that will present previously unthought-of ideas. This can lead to wholly new directions that have complete backing and enthusiastic support from everyone involved.

For example, we worked with a small construction company in Denver. The leadership was unconvinced about the staying power of sustainable building practices but since their principle client was government; they were not seeing a strong interest there.

After two and a half days of hearing from invited stakeholders and engaging in discussions with all aspects of their employees, investors, and clients, the slowing down of government contracts, coupled with the vast amount of private commercial buildings that needed to be retrofitted to meet the sustainable guidelines of the Federal government, they decided to turn around 360 degrees and embrace a totally different business model.

Not only that, there evolved a deep discussion about the ethical issues inherent in the 'lowest bidder' process. The result was an intention to start a separate company where all of the local contractors could get together to make the case for changes in the bidding process to both government and private clients. Who could have predicted that? Working collaboratively often reaps unexpected results that far exceed expectations!

Some potential issues in planning collaboratively include having the courage and the willingness to appear vulnerable to participants as real information is shared and questions are encouraged. The enthusiastic momentum needs to be maintained after the meeting, or cynicism will set in which is hard to counter. It takes gumption to allow the 2-3 days this kind of planning needs. That often seems way too much time at the start and not enough at the end.

Their Relationship

You can look at Strategic Planning as vision work. While it will include the start of the implementation, many of the daily actions and tactics will be developed later, and this is where the business plan comes into being. The business plan is much more strongly tied to mission. Together they form a very strong and clear direction, but you won't really know where you are going unless you get outside of your own head. What I find sad is that you *can* do one without the other. You can have success in doing so, but the *level* of success cannot be reached without both. You can get to Louisiana by car or by plane. The view is different and the timeframe is different, but if you go by car it is hard to understand what you missed by not going by plane and vice versa.

Choosing

Which should you do first? If you have investor needs that can determine the business plan then do the collaborative strategic planning first - and invite your investors. You will go from prosaic to awesome.

If you are a small business owner with few or no employees, go with the business plan, if you can only do one. You will have a clear road map that will serve you well.

If you are a small business with 20 or more employees, go with the collaborative strategic plan, if you can only do one. You will generate clarity and enthusiasm that will carry through to implementation, if you let it. You will also get ahead of the pack in a way you never would have dreamed of before.

No, I'm not a fan of traditional strategic planning - collaboration is the only way to go! Collaboration is systemic and gives you a much better chance to see the whole picture. Seeing wholes is a big part of sustainable intelligence and collaboration is a good way to get there.

Systems Thinking and the Wisconsin Thing

What does Systems Thinking have to do with Union busting? One of the major principles of living systems is that information is needed from all parts of the system. That is why unions are necessary! Like all aspects of a system, when one part of the system feels like they know it all and does not listen to the rest of the system, then we have problems. These are truisms folks and apply to ALL aspects of living systems.

We confuse problems with where they surface and 'blame' instead of looking for structural issues (can't get information from another part, for instance) that might be causing those issues. When we think parts and pieces, we act like Don Quixote and tilt at windmills instead of actually solving problems.

In Wisconsin, the budget maybe a problem, but the deficit wasn't caused by one part of the system and weakening the system won't solve the problem either. It *may* remove a presenting symptom, but that symptom will recur later in another area. That other area will then get 'blamed' for being a problem - you get the picture.

The national budget is no different and neither is *your* internal budget.

Seeing from a systems point of view gets to the root cause of problems and stops the name-calling and finger pointing that only generates ill will and perpetuates things. Each aspect of the system holds an important truth. Until that truth is seen and acknowledged, nothing done will be effective or final. Until reality is dealt with, no progress is achieved - we just keep spinning our wheels.

If we really want to move on and get over our delight in the emotional drama, then we need to learn to listen and really hear the truth in what others are saying. If the truth is not apparent (and in emotional language it often is not) then we need to ask questions. Getting to why others are angry or afraid is much more important and meaningful than just knowing that they feel that way.

Asking questions also addresses the manipulative aspect created by emotional blackmail. If we work to appease instead of understand, we remain trapped in the same

unworkable situation that we are striving to
address.

This is a leadership issue and it takes a
person who is willing to acknowledge and deal
with their own shadow to be able to create a
culture that is open to exploring the deeply
meaningful aspects of work that really drive
people to do their best, but the results are worth
it!

Sustainable Intelligence - Business Transformation

There are SO many lessons business can
learn by paying attention to how nature works. So
much of the current approach to sustainability has
to do with lack and with using less, for we are
blind to the treasures and richness with which
nature abounds.

Nature is nothing if not prolific. The
beauty of ancient and untouched landscapes is a
wonder of verdant lushness and productivity. The
bounty that nature provides is awe-inspiring.
Equally awe-inspiring is our lack of respect and
appreciation for it.

One of my most inspiring memories was a visit to Hartwick Forest in Michigan. This track of forest has never been cut. You could see for miles under the trees, as nothing could grow in the many feet of pine needles under the trees. The ground was soft and easy to walk on, making moccasins a realistic choice for shoes. I could only imagine what America must have looked like to the early visitors from Europe. And then I look at what it's like right now and it is equally hard to imagine how we could have been so blind and greedy!

The message I have for business is not about lack, but about verdurous, lushness, and plenty. The hitch is that to bring back and make use of the prolific essence of nature, we need to act differently than we do now. Behavior change is never a welcome thought, yet we often make changes in our lives, both for personal reasons and because of circumstances, so there is no reason to believe that we can't do so now. Especially when the benefits are so huge.

Companies that take up these kinds of changes now before the pressures of rising prices of resources, force change will not only have a head start, but also a much easier time. Many of these changes take time, so the early adopters will definitely be the winners!

I wish we would listen to our hearts and pay attention to our behavior. We go for drives in the country, not through the nearest subdivision. We take vacations to the mountains and the seaside and come back refreshed. When trees are planted in cities, the crime goes down. Surely this tells us something about our feelings and *need* for nature. Yet we are planning uranium mines near the Grand Canyon and copper mines at the last pristine headwater for wild salmon. The Hartwick Forest website did not have even one photo of the trees - we do not appreciate what we have!

The real fundamental change that is needed is one that each of us has to make. We need to *care*. We need to care more than we fear. We need to care more than we *want*. We have to reconnect our hearts to our minds and *act as if we cared*.

⨖

Final Thoughts

As business people and entrepreneurs we tend to be driven by the latest crisis. This one pointed, but very limited perspective gets the crisis solved (maybe) but opens us up to additional issues that seem to come out of nowhere.

By training ourselves to see wholes instead of just parts and pieces, we can begin to recognize the larger picture and plan ahead thus saving ourselves from doing constant remediation so we can actually get ahead.

5 Culture – the Invisible Asset

"Treat people as if they were what they ought to be, and you help them to become what they are capable of being." ~
Johann Wolfgang von Goethe

Culture – How we are Connected

How we work together determines the kind of success we can achieve. It also determines how satisfied we are with our work and our work experience. It assures us that our contributions are meaningful or leaves us resentful and cynical at the end of the day. Culture is what lets us leave a legacy or what makes us grateful that we can finally quit. So much of our life is all about how well we fit into the culture we have at work. If our work doesn't support us then we either shrivel up or find satisfaction in other things. Poor cultures are debilitating, good cultures are invigorating and empowering.

The Sustainable Values Set® provides a blueprint for the creation of a life-enhancing culture, a culture that brings out the best in people and that makes the best possible for the organization. The deep appreciation and the strong sense of US that results from using the Sustainable Values Set® as a decision-making tool, is also the kind of environment that assures people of their value by supporting them in contributing at their highest and best.

WHAT'S IT MEAN – SHIFTING TO GREEN?

Creating a Sustainable Culture: Lessons from Apple

The whole point of sustainable business strategies is to have a long-term impact. A company cannot achieve this goal without a culture that is aligned with these sustainable goals. So what is a sustainable culture and how do you achieve one? One big hurdle to achieving deep green sustainability is the commitment and will to do so accompanied by capacity for the innovation that's necessary to succeed. This is sort of a chicken and egg situation. You need people actively engaged in experimentation with a strong streak of self-initiative to see the promise and benefits gained from mimicking nature, and you also need these same capabilities to take advantage of the models nature offers.

Apple is an excellent example of being proactive in supporting people to change. Yes, they sell products and we Americans are very well trained to buy the newest and best, but the difference between the PC and Mac worlds can be daunting for most people. To address this they have done two major things right: 1) they absolutely and completely support people making the change, 2) they have a culture that empowers employees to learn, grow and experiment to continually improve the customer experience. The two go hand-in-hand.

Can your company learn from this? First, ask yourself how easy is it to learn? How easy is it to access training? How easy is it to actually use that training? How easy is it to access support materials and refresher courses? How often do your employees share their new ideas and insights with each other? A series of alternative questions might be: What happens when employees fail? What happens when mistakes are made? How often do employees share mistakes? Is training mandatory or available upon request? What are the rules about the kinds of training that employees can get and who makes those decisions? Long-term sustainable business practices will remain out of reach if management insists on controlling what's going on. It used to be that one of the differences between management and leadership was the difference between control and attention to direction/strategy and vision. It used to be that was a difference between telling and monitoring.

I don't believe that those differences exist in companies that are moving forward and embracing the changes that are everywhere. The driving need to have a responsive, adaptive and resilient organization requires a responsive, adaptive and flexible workforce, one that learns on its feet and that can respond in a nano second to changing circumstances. If your management can't handle this, then your employees sure can't.

Learn from Apple and make work fun and exciting. Ensure that your employees have an opportunity to learn something new everyday. Set up processes to handle the routine and release your people to explore the spontaneous, new and growth- producing opportunities that will take your company into the future – sustainably!

Response to the Harvard Business Review Blog: Building a Resilient Organizational Culture *by George S. Everly, Jr.*

My comments:

I enjoyed your article. In my work resilience is seen as a normal part of natural systems, so we have looked at human systems from the natural perspective. We see creativity and innovation as the parents of resilience, so that any leadership behavior that fosters these will also support resilience. Your four: optimism, decisiveness, integrity and open communication are interesting. We would see integrity as a commitment to the integrity of the whole and a commitment to serving ALL life.

Open communication is key to any system's self-learning and self-organization when its core is committed to resilience. Decisiveness is simply taking action and can be experimentation as well as commitment. Optimism is really about the joy we see in life, yes? When we are able to play (experiment), contribute, have our value acknowledged, then optimism is not hard to come by. Thank you for an interesting article.

In my work applying the wisdom of natural systems to human ones (business to be specific) the availability of information is key to self-organization - a core aspect of group resilience. This is one place most companies can make clear and fast improvements. Optimism would support seeing the possibilities in that information.

In my work I have framed integrity as Integrity of the Whole for a very specific reason.

Resilience is about adapting to the external environment in a way that supports the ENTIRE system into more robust health. We often miss that piece, and integrity, as usually spoken about is a reference to individual integrity - useful, necessary even, but not at the expense of the larger system. Humans have reached a point where we need to be conscious of the larger system and act with concern for its health. This is a new situation and one at the root of the various crises we now face.

The ability to make decisions is simply the ability to act. I prefer the term self-organization as it more accurately reflects the kind of decision-making and where that decision-making takes place. We are very addicted to having a 'leader' and seeking protection behind someone or something. The shift to self-organization is another key aspect of this shift and why resilience cannot rest in the 'leadership.' During a crisis leadership may come from surprising places so the ability to allow the wisdom and skills residing in the system as a whole to come to the fore is crucial to resilience.

Culture and Sustainability

For over 15 years I've worked on and with culture. Culture in organizations is the bedrock of beliefs that determine what behavior employees see as both possible and beneficial. The bottom line is that if behavior is not seen as beneficial (to the employees) then anything requiring that kind of behavior is believed to be *not possible*.

This is why I'm so keen on matching the strategic needs important to a company's future with the culture. Ask anyone and they will tell you stories of companies that have created strategic plans, only to have them sit on the shelf. One reason why is that the behaviors needed to implement that strategy did not live in the culture.

If the new strategy required innovation for example, and employees have been systematically restricted from experimenting, if their suggestions have been ignored, or if mistakes and failures are severely punished, then no employee will really believe that the leadership wants innovation and no one will take the risks needed to make innovation happen.

As companies move toward sustainability this becomes even more important. One of the

key benefits of strategic sustainability efforts is the
generation of new ways of thinking and working
that lead to innovative processes, products and
revenue streams. If the culture of the organization
does not lend itself to creativity and
experimentation, then the deeper and more
strategic aspects of sustainability will not resonate.

Additionally, if the goal is to put
sustainability into the DNA of the organization,
then a major piece of that process is the
revamping of the company culture. The
Triplepundent talks about the 'value' employee,
one for whom the connection between personal
values and company values is key. This
connection will reduce turnover, attract more
capable employees, and generate a sense of
empowerment that increases productivity. This is
the holy grail of culture – a cemented connection
between the beliefs and values of the employees
with the strategic needs of the company. When
these two meet magic happens!

The Network for Business Sustainability in
a recent report says, "93% of CEOs see
sustainability as important to their company's
future success. Yet, most do not know how to
embed sustainability into their company." Culture

has always been an opaque subject to those who are used to dealing with tangible and easily measureable objects. This was the reason I have worked so hard to create tools that measure culture and that offer companies a way to determine the depth of leadership understanding and how well their management style evokes desired behavior in employees.

As we move forward in greening our businesses, we will need to make some serious shifts in how we manage if we wish to see the extraordinary benefits gained from 'thinking like the planet' manifest in increased profit and reduced costs. This is the direction we are going and this is where the true benefits of being Deep Green will manifest themselves!

Corporate Social Responsibility Wave of the Future?

I was going through the website for the Corporate Citizenship Conference and the various video clips submitted by organizations on their corporate citizenship projects. Corporations are going all over the world to help people in developing nations in many ways. It is heartwarming to see the good that companies can do if they try.

From a sustainability perspective there are several ethical issues with this that bother me. I have a personal problem with our being a "do gooder." We in the Western world think our lifestyle is the best and often our approach to 'helping' is to change the lifestyle of developing nations to match our own. Now we all know where that is going ... we can't sustain our own lifestyle so moving others into the same wasteful and unsustainable habits is not exactly a recipe for long-term success.

I know we feel guilty about not letting others in on the 'best' way to live, but maybe that is actually our arrogance talking. Maybe that attitude is the rationale for 1) not really paying attention to how others live, 2) a cover up for making us feel comfortable about why we don't make any changes, 3) embarrassment in having to learn from others 'less fortunate' than ourselves.

Most of these countries have managed to live the same way for thousands of years, while we've only been at it for about 200. Who is the wiser? Yes they have to deal with drought, famine, disease and war, but they are often actually happier than we are when measured on the <u>Gross Happiness Index</u>. We all know that stuff doesn't make us happy, but that doesn't seem to change our behavior any.

The ethical issues I see are several: we tell and don't listen; we try to 'save' instead of facilitate; we introduce methods that are not sustainable, thus pushing developing countries into the same unsustainable ways of thinking and living that currently threaten our planet; we don't see ourselves as equals and therefore make the interactions mutual, i.e. we do not learn and change our own behavior, thus setting up an artificial hierarchy with us on top.

Reciprocity is a key value in natural systems. Everything is interconnected and therefore everything contributes, even as it receives. This means that receiving is as important as giving. In Western societies however, giving is seen as better and so becomes a way to manipulate and control instead of being a way in which relationships are enriched. This is our poverty!

Final Thoughts

Culture maybe invisible, but is far from powerless. Our attitude that it is "just business" gives us permission to deny our morality. *This* is something that must change.

෧

6 Leadership for the Long Term

I don't know what your destiny will be, but one thing I do know: the only ones among you who will be really happy are those who have sought and found how to serve. ~**Albert Schweitzer**, *philosopher, physician, musician, Nobel laureate (1875-1965)*

We're Not in Kansas Anymore...

Different times require different actions.
You know the definition of insanity, "Doing the
same thing over and over, but expecting different
results." Different results require leadership that
can make that happen. Over the past 50 years
we've gone from discussions about leadership -
born or bred, innate or learned to servant
leadership and transformational leadership. As the
need has changed from getting people to do what
you want to getting the best from them, we have
begun to make the connection between leadership
style and employee actions.

Now as the situation has changed the need
for speed and innovation from the workforce has
never been greater. There is something else
though, that is different this time. Up to now we
have been trying to do the same things except
better, faster, cheaper. Now we need to do
entirely different things.

Our outlook as a human species has been
human centric. That was correct when we
struggled for survival and fought for food, but the
impact we've had on our home is now raising its

ugly head and the sight is enough to give a strong man pause!

The deep rethinking now taking place as we begin to see ourselves having an actual role in the evolution of our home is scary, ambiguous, completely new and 360 degrees from how we have understood our role in the past. This is very new territory!

Leaders in this new sustainable world will have to love the planet as passionately as they do their employees, their company and their nation! They will have to be able to see the bigger picture, understand non-linear cause and effect, work *with* nature's principles and processes, *and* ensure that employees do that too. This is not about the man in the white hat riding in to rescue those in distress - this is about the creation of communities that learn together how to achieve success *and at the same time make the Earth better for their presence.* This is a tall order!

Illusion of Leadership: How Sustainable Leadership is Different

We have been seduced by the thought that leadership means that the person designated as "leader" does something that makes others want to do something too. The corollary is that others don't want to do anything and wouldn't if it wasn't for the leader.

What if that wasn't true? What if the others really, really wanted to do something? Consider for a moment if *you* might be an "other," do *you* want to do something? Do *you* have dreams and desires? Do *you* think you just might have solutions to some problems you see everyday? Do you?

So, if others *do* have dreams, desires and possible solutions, what role does the leader play?

What if "leader" was a job description much like teacher, or mentor or janitor? If Leadership were a job title, what would the job description look like? Hmmm, maybe a little like teacher, a little like mentor, a little like coach, and a little like trailblazer, and maybe just a little like scout? Maybe the leader's job is to evoke from the others their innate abilities, dreams and desires?

Maybe the leader is really a cheerleader with vision?

That leads to another seduction. Leaders often think that the job title means they can do whatever they want. They have dreams, desires and potential solutions that they really, really want to try out. Good on them! What that usually comes with however, is the whining about the others. Stories about how *they* don't understand, how *they* won't follow through and don't really care, and that what they do or want to do won't last.

This seduction is most often seen in organizations where the leadership changes about every 4-5 years for top leaders and about every two years for up and coming stars.

Michael Watkins surveyed Fortune 500 company HR Directors and found that executives had an average tenure of 4 years; high potential managers 2 1/2 - 3 years. In his book, he quotes Brad Smart as saying that the cost of a failed executive hire was 24 times base compensation.

This is expensive in every way. The constant yanking around means that leaders, who believe this seduction strive to make their own mark at the cost of the organization's progress. This becomes a never-ending cycle, one that organizations survive in spite of the turmoil it causes.

In some organizations and in many governmental roles, tenure is mandated (think term limits) with the belief that change will prevent corruption. This process has become so ingrained that leadership succession is almost mandated in some companies.

Organizations that continually rotate leaders select those that can "get their way" the fastest. The focus on manipulative power, political cunning and strong will have more to say about the character of the person than about their ability to serve and build the organization, but it is these that get promoted!

These two seductions create a lazy approach to leadership. It is way easier to try and get your own way than it is to listen and hear what the collective is saying. History is littered with leaders including kings and others who tried to go against the will of the people and paid dearly. It is much easier to frighten and cajole, manipulate and outsmart than it is to erase self-doubt, clarify vision and believe in others even when they don't believe in themselves.

We are not taught collaborative techniques to work and play together, we are taught competitive techniques that keep us separate and reinforce the belief that one someone is better than everyone else.

Knowing these seductions and being able to address them is critical as we move into sustainable business practices. The pressing need for organizations to be flexible and resilient, the demand for innovation that is off the charts, all call for a leadership that is skilled in evoking the very best from others. This kind of shift cannot be done by one person - no matter how skilled and forceful. In fact force is the opposite of innovation it is an expression of fear, not experimentation, trust or curiosity - all components of creativity and innovation.

The ability to be collaborative, to evoke the best from others and to create a culture of excited experimentation and innovation are the hallmarks of the new sustainable leadership and are the new measures of a leader practicing sustainable intelligence.

Managing Change for Long-Term Success

One often unmentioned aspect of implementing sustainable business practices is managing change. When sustainability is seen as a strategic direction, then the entire organization must play a part. Deep Green sustainability will impact everything the business does and in ways largely unanticipated.

The formulation of an environmental plan is just the first step. The actualizing of it provides both fun and excitement, but it also can lead the company into unexpected areas creating new pressures. As an organization grapples with the internal changes there are also external changes (such as a search for new vendors, client communication, etc.) that undo old practices and relationships. Because of the large number of potential changes and impacts, an effective implementation of a well developed environmental plan goes way beyond the scope of any one manager and will tap many resources that have been previously undeveloped. Like any other system-wide change, leadership and communication become key. What makes this approach to change different is the wonderful and inspiring stories that bubble up as employees generate creative approaches to solve problems.

These stories are inspiring and motivating in ways that few other approaches to change can offer. Sharing them both internally and externally is one of the key aspects of an effective change process.

The autonomy and freedom to experiment that employee's need is another unusual aspect of a successful implementation to a sustainable approach to business. Because of the ambiguity in finding immediate solutions, employees need increased freedom to experiment and strategize when trying to solve problems for which there maybe few or no ready solutions.

When sustainability becomes a strategic direction then the company may find that they are stepping out ahead of the normal suppliers to their industry, so new relationships and transitioning practices need to be developed. Becoming Deep Green is not an event - it is a journey. The commitment to that journey has to be tied to strategy or the will may weaken and the pull to get back to doing business as usual can get the upper hand.

Learning about the unique complexities of sustainable leadership can help committed organizations identify and address many of these issues before they become problems.

Humans are hard-wired for learning and too often our jobs become humdrum and we lose that edge. Those companies that take on a strong commitment to sustainability will find that it generates an enthusiasm and excitement that few other projects can because of the learning and discovery inherent in looking at the business with new eyes.

Sustainable Leadership and Fiscal Responsibility

One of the key attributes of sustainable leadership is fiscal responsibility, but it may not look like what you think.

My heart went out to Japan and I ached for the pain of their tragedy as the tsunamis shocked the world! The shock and loss are staggering. The pain however was just starting. While the pain of personal emotional and financial loss are hard to bear the nuclear explosions in the damaged reactors hinted at more trials in the near future.

During that time car and computer chip manufacturing were stopped. No one knew for how long. As a leading world supplier of these the ripples were felt worldwide. The resulting loss of wages to employees and income to companies was another impact of some magnitude in many countries, not just Japan.

The financial cost of just repairing the damage will be huge, not to mention the cost of any nuclear clean up or health issues. Japan has been struggling to get out of their own economic woes for a decade and I have to wonder how these additional financial burdens will impact that. This disaster is a living example of systems thinking as the interconnectedness of our world becomes apparent.

Look at these photos - move the center bar to see the whole picture, and ask yourself how much of this can a country stand? How long will it take Japan to recover? Is thinking about these kinds of things in the best national / personal interest? Can effects of events of this size be mitigated? Planning needs to take into account these new realities.

Normally fiscal responsibility would be seen as doing much of what Japan did: the country has a high level of preparedness for disaster; their nuclear reactors were built to withstand earth quakes; the government is trained and prepared to step in and help. All of these are good.

By using a planning methodology that includes an awareness of the natural world and likely responses, sustainable leaders are able to think ahead of tragedy and truly plan for the future. By committing to *sustainable* approaches the temptation to address pressing needs with short-term solutions is diminished.

Perhaps, using sustainable leadership, people would have the foresight to see the fiscal consequences of putting many nuclear facilities in one place, over or near fault lines and close to a tsunami prone coastline. Maybe the knowledge and respect for Mother Nature would prevent the rationalizing that only a 7.9 quake could possibly happen. Maybe.

My intent is to point out the very different kinds of thinking that using a sustainable approach offers, with the very sad example of that tragedy being used for comparison.

It's not possible to change the past, but we can act to change the future. We need to do so *before* things of this magnitude happen again. The problem of course, is that we want to believe that this is something that only happens every 800 years or so. We *want* to believe it is a freak of nature, but think back to the past few years and how many freaks of nature have we experienced? What do you *really* think the future offers? If we don't respect the power of which the Earth is capable *and* act from that respect, then we will have learned nothing from the past few years.

WE *have* to begin to think differently, act differently and plan differently!

Leadership Practices and Green Business

It is customary for corporations to rotate people they are grooming for leadership positions. The rotation gives them exposure and experience to various aspects of the business - and it does. But it also means that companies are selecting for leadership traits that may not be in their best interest.

If managing a budget is important, then I can beat my numbers for about two years if I don't repair, train or invest. If percentages of increase in production or sales are important, then I can beat my numbers by driving my people, forcing them to 'get creative'. Shipping bricks and substandard product is a good way to get the numbers! By the time the dust settles the boss has moved on and tracking the source of the issue can be moot.

What gets measured is what gets done, but if the measures push unintended consequences, then they can do more harm than good. End game measures - how much, at what cost and when the task is completed. All of these are subject to distortion and provide no feedback for improvement. Percentage of improvement on the other hand, is a 'living' measure that drives results.

Are your measures selecting for leaders who are heavy-handed, manipulative and punitive? Are you relying more on force, cleverness or fear to drive your company than curiosity, learning and collaboration?

Because being Green is new territory, there is no one answer, and in most cases the solutions to vexing problems actually have to be invented. It is not possible to achieve lasting success using old fashioned and top-down tactics.

This means that force has to be replaced with meaning and commitment; fear with curiosity and experimentation; and manipulation with collaboration. These are hard changes to make if fear is the keystone management tool. The creation of a flexible and resilient culture is essential to creating a sustainable business.

There is a subtle resistance to sustainability and this is a profound mistake because the benefits can put you on the map and make you an industry leader, if you are an early adopter. The solutions are often not apparent and will not be achieved by traditional methods. Shifting the leadership and culture to generate the appropriate answers for each unique business requires time and practice - lots of practice. The longer a company waits the more pressure there will be, and the fewer options that will be available. Waiting also means that the leadership status gained by being an early adopter goes to someone else.

Start-ups and those with an entrepreneurial mindset have a unique opportunity here. All of these things are easier at the beginning. I spent some time chatting with Scott Tibbits, the founder of Starsys Research and he shared with me that he spent hours thinking about how he would interface with employees before he even started his company. That is a remarkable statement from an entrepreneur, but he was able to build a business that put rockets into space and that was acquired in 2005 by SpaceDev. True to form he paid considerable attention to the cultures of both companies before agreeing to the merger, something that few CEOs do in any field. Now Scott may be an unusual man, but the lessons he teaches can be learned by anyone and they are particularly germane for companies going green.

Together – at Last?

This year is one of relationship for me. When we believe we are separate, we struggle; we blame and often feel overwhelmed. How would you rank yourself in the areas of finances, relationships, health and spirituality? Give yourself a 1 (low) to 5 (high) on each. No matter what area is lowest, in every case that score can be improved through relationships!

If we had as many words for love as the Eskimos did for snow, then we would not have this issue. We see relationships as simple things or over the top complicated. We basically have two words for relationship – hard or soft. In business the 'soft' stuff is disdained, but that is actually where we are the least experienced, the least competent, the least confident.

We do poorly what we do least. Why? Because we need practice, practice, practice, but instead we quit when the going gets rough. We quit and then whine because we can't get what we think we deserve or ardently desire. Surely that keeps God rolling on the floor laughing!

We don't relate well to our families, our spouses, our kids, our employees, our vendors, our clients or even ourselves. We are clueless when it comes to managing our expectations. Our expectations become secret contracts that only we have signed, then those contracts give us permission to judge and convict the other party for their imaginary agreement. Again I can see God laughing until there are tears in her eyes.

Everything your business needs comes through people. So join me, make this the year of relationships. Smile at those you work with, tell them what makes you so glad they are who they are. Take a moment to say, "thanks" or "great job." Make a phone call, write a card, just stop by - let employees know that you recognize them and how they contribute.

Ask an employee's advice, ask how they did what they did and what you can do to help. Take time for the 'soft' stuff this year, then next year rank yourself again in finances, relationships, health and spirituality and see where you stand.

Sustainable Leadership

We call her Mother, but think about how we treat her. Sustainable leadership is about healing this possibly lethal sickness. In looking over some of the photos provided by National Geographic of the Earth from space, I could not help but wonder why we don't appreciate our home.

Our minds get all fogged up about who's to blame, we wonder why these changes are happening and our emotions scream why do *I* have to change, why do *I* have to be inconvenienced, why *me?* All the while our clever thoughts rationalize our behavior so we are comfortable continuing on as before.

What will it take to shift us into action? What will it take for each of us to step into the leadership role we were born into but conveniently sidestep? When will we see and when will we say, "Enough?"

As business struggles to become sustainable, we are experiencing a leadership crisis like never before. Who is stepping up to the plate to make the personal changes everyone must make? Who is creating the path that all of us must follow?

The courage it takes is not just about stepping into the unknown; we will be forced into that. It is not just about the uncertainty of action or the long time it takes to see results. The courage is about seeing clearly both the situation and our contributions to it. Having courage is about facing the truth about ourselves and forgiving ourselves so we can move forward. The past is past and we need to be strong enough to act differently more than we ever have before. Shame, guilt and denial all suck the energy we need to get on with life.

With few exceptions most of us didn't know. We didn't understand what we were doing. Denial is just a way of pretending we weren't and aren't responsible. The truth however, is that we are. We don't have to be the ones to blame; in fact no blame needs to be placed. But being responsible is a good thing, for what we've done we can undo – IF we can forgive ourselves and accept the responsibility for change.

The illusion we labor under is that of the ostrich - if it is not seen it does not exist. We laugh at the cartoon, but ignore the similarities in our own behavior. We need leaders with courage - will you be one?

✌

Final Thoughts

Leaders, in particular need to take the long view! We look for trends and use some of our number gathering to try and spot trends, but the patterns in human behavior and nature seem to elude us. We see cycles in nature, but the patterns made by little changes that happen continuously over time and that lead to big changes, are invisible.

Out tendency to see things as unconnected and 'one offs' mislead us into thinking we are safe in making change, when we are just making more work and doing long-term damage. Change is a fact of life, but not understanding interconnections destroys the internal networks that make our workforce effective when we downsize, as well increasing costs through unmanaged waste.

Learning to discern patterns and see wholes is a key leadership skill!

~

7 The Economics of Sustainability

We basically have three choices: mitigation, adaptation and suffering. We're going to do some of each. The question is what the mix is going to be. The more mitigation we do, the less adaptation will be required and the less suffering there will be. ~**John Holden**

The Cost of Sustainability

There is a lot of concern being expressed that sustainable business practices are expensive and a fear that tampering with those industries that are in trouble or causing trouble will be bad for the economy. A large part of market dynamics has to do with seeing businesses come and go, rise and fall, start up and fold. We have allowed some businesses to get so big and so entangled in every aspect of our lives that the personal discomfort we will experience as things shift has made people personally wary.

In sports there is the saying, "No pain, no gain" and that appears to be true for the economic changes that need to happen to bring the economy back to health. Like a person who has faced death – life will not be the same after. The current economy was developed without much conscious thought. The intent that was applied was done by special interest groups and done without thought about the health of the whole.

This is a different time and we now know much more about how economic dynamics function. We also have other models (nature, for instance) that offer different constructs and that have a history of being effective for the whole, that we were not aware of in the past. This makes me optimistic that there is a chance we can get it right. At the very least we can begin to move in the right direction. Doing so will require the courage to face the reality we've made and the ability to forgive ourselves coupled with the commitment to care deeply about all life on this big blue ball we call home.

Market issues and a Sustainable Economy

With corporations discovering the value of sustainable business practices, it is time to bring the benefits of sustainability to the broader economy. Business prospers when the larger economy resets its priorities to ensure a robust middle class, when stable and transparent financial markets exist, when an educated workforce is available and when investments are made in maintaining a reliable transportation, energy and communications infrastructure—all fundamental to a sustainable economy.

Without good sustainability policies, the economy suffers economic damage (such as bank bailouts, high unemployment and massive environmental cleanups), which lead to greater federal deficits, depleted local and state treasuries, reduced services and higher costs to businesses and consumers, suppressing demand and profits. The remedial actions required to clean up these disasters is wasteful. This is not a good use of funds and takes funds away from those emerging business practices that will create the jobs and long-term employment needed for the future.

One of the key failures of the market has been the distortion in price that is achieved by the externalization of costs. Hazel Henderson in 1996 in her book, *Creating Alternative Futures: the end of economics* was among the first to sound the alarm. "These costs get pushed around the system until they can be forced into some other group's balance sheet or hidden in environmental degradation or pushed forward to future generations." She was followed in 2002 by William McDonough and Michael Braungart in their book, *Cradle to Cradle: rethinking how we make things*. They made the case that an industrial system that "takes, makes and wastes" cannot become a creator of goods and services that generate ecological, social and economic value. It has been over twenty years and these are lessons we still have to learn.

Subsidies are another market distortion. In spite of the rhetoric about a 'free market' the market is anything but free.

"Once we subsidize, the pricing structure is no longer true. It is even worse for items such as petrol and other sources of energy for which pricing often in turn determines the prices of other than goods and services. When the pricing of a fundamental item or a service is not true, the retail prices of everything related to the subsidized items or services become artificial. In the end, we have an artificial economy. And we know that anything artificial lasts relatively shorter than their genuine counterparts."

Mustapha Kamil, Executive Editor of Business at the Business Times.

Harry Mosier, voted into the 2010 World Manufacturing Hall of Fame, Chairman of the Reshoring Institute and Chairman Emeritus of Agie Charmilles, believes that on a macroeconomic level, re-shoring bolsters the U.S.

manufacturing and defense base, creates jobs and reduces the trade and budget deficits. But Mosier also believes there's an increasingly strong business case for bringing outsourced manufacturing work back to domestic soil, which he summarizes as a lower "total cost of ownership." Offshoring functions in very similar way to subsidies, in that it shifts the burden of cost and undermines the system as a whole.

Democracy - in business? What a concept. Russel Ackoff, Professor Emeritus at MIT first mentioned that this might be a good idea in 1995. David Brodwin, co-founder of The New Economy Network and the American Sustainability Business Council (ASBC) and member of the board has been active around the issue of the recent Supreme Court Decision, Citizens United, which has effectively *limited* the voice of the majority of small business voices as well as individual citizens, feels the understanding of democracy as the *voice of the people* would lead to a participative and collaborative style of management in business organizations. Most of our organizations function with those deemed 'leadership' having a larger and often the only voice. This is exactly the situation David sees occurring, on a national basis, from the Citizens United decision.

The White House and Congress can do their part to address these issues as there are several policy issues that must to be addressed at this level; the elimination of tax breaks for off shoring and tax havens, affordable funding for small businesses, choices in business forms that prevent penalties for working for the greater good, the revitalization of domestic manufacturing, the setting of national standards for sustainable business practices, and stimulating the economy are all areas for Federal action. Do you think the government will act on these issues effectively?

Sustainability and Capitalism

Are the missions of sustainability and green business in opposition to capitalism? There are those who think so and those who embrace Conscious Capitalism and Sustainable Capitalism as a statement about where Capitalism is and should go. Ann Charles, blogging for FastCompany said in her blog: "Mr. Haque makes the point in The Capitalist's Paradox that what's standing in the way of great capitalism today might just be yesterday's capitalists--"trying at every turn to stifle competition, squelch information, earn an unfair advantage, and extract value from people, nature, and the future, instead of creating authentic, thick, shared value for them."

That sure sounds like the belief system that has gotten us into this trouble, all right. It's what happens when the fear of scarcity activates our survival instincts and when we really and truly believe that we only have to worry about our own / personal survival. That sense of separation coupled with, "no one's the boss of me" attitude lends itself very well to a justification of power over, manipulation and even greed as a survival mechanism.

Sustainable Capitalism as promulgated by Al Gore and David Blood and explained in the book: *Sustainable Capitalism: A Matter of Common Sense* by John Ikerd and others seeks to give Capitalism the long-term perspective it sorely lacks. They also grapple with the issue of value and seek to tie financial gain to the creation of real and lasting value. This approach focuses on transparency and measure as a means to ensure business takes into account the needs of the entire planet. Conscious Capitalism, as supported by John Mackey of Whole Foods and Kip Tindell of The Container Store among others, and the Conscious Capitalism Institute defines itself by saying, "Conscious Capitalists are unapologetic advocates for free markets, entrepreneurship, competition, freedom to trade, property rights, freedom to contract, and the rule of law. They recognize that these are essential elements of a healthy, functioning economy, as are trust, compassion, collaboration, and value-creation." A question Libertarians have to address is whether property rights trump nature's rights. That said, they are much more values-focused, particularly in their concerns about leadership.

"Conscious leadership means to be consciously awake. To lead consciously means to be authentic, to be aware of the implications of one's decisions, including a commitment to ongoing learning and personal growth. Conscious Leaders adopt a holistic worldview that moves beyond the limitations of traditional machine metaphors for business. They view their enterprises as part of a complex, interdependent, and evolving system with multiple constituencies. Conscious Leaders see that profit is one of the important outcomes of the business, but not the sole purpose. Most importantly, they reject a zero-sum, trade-off oriented view of business and look for creative synergistic win-win approaches that offer multiple kinds of value simultaneously to all stakeholders."

At the heart of both approaches is the need to shift people's behavior in ways that work within the rhythms and boundaries of nature. The Sustainable Values Set®, by making nature's approach to sustaining life available for everyday decision-making, provides a framework that ensures intent and actions align. The heart of this value set is the kernel at the core of nature's behavior – all actions create the conditions that support life.

If all of the decisions a business made were made to ensure Life (not just existence, but the *joy* in existence) then a better, healthy and sustainable world would be close at hand!

Sustainability, Alternative Energy and Economics

My mind boggles when people include nuclear in the alternative energy options. The argument is that sustainability is best served when our energy sources do not contribute to the carbon load on the Earth. They are absolutely right that non-carbon forms of energy are needed.

Stewart Brand of Whole Earth catalogue fame has come out in favor of nuclear power to help avert climate impact by carbon. I think fear makes us silly. I also think that we fear because we have no faith in our own powers of invention and creativity. We forget that it is boundaries that stimulate creativity - limits are our friends!

But let's talk economics for a minute. Toshiba Corp., one of the suppliers for four of Fukushima's six reactors, along with three other companies has given an estimate of the cost and timeline for decommissioning these plants. They are projecting 10 years and hundreds of millions of dollars to address the contamination and long-term protection needed. Other similar plants with fewer problems have taken $950 million and are likely to exceed 1 billion and Gunderson thinks the Fukushima cost will run many times that.

Given that there is a half-life of 24,000 years, and the 'safe' sealing off and monitoring of the plant while the radiation inside decays, is done with concrete and a slab underneath to prevent seepage, a process that doesn't sound very 'safe' to me, what's the real cost? Heavily contaminated areas would be entombed in concrete. The best solution is to entomb the site for 40, 50, 60 years according to Arnold Gunderson, a man who wrote part of the manual on decommissioning (per the Associated Press). Sixty years and the half-life again is...?

Is anyone including these externalized costs in the price of nuclear? No, only cost for construction and maintenance are included in the figures that get tossed around as the 'cost of nuclear power.' So we have not only the horrible cost of contamination, but also the cost of decommissioning and the cost of waste processing and storage. Is the trade off die now or later? That sounds like a Faustian bargain to me.

Externalities are something we forget in many areas. The true cost of coal would shift if the externalities were included and it would no longer be 'cheap.' We love our illusions, but we are only fooling ourselves - who do you think pays for this? Not the manufacturers of the cost, you can bet on that.

Externalities are key to understanding the real economic arguments, and understanding them helps prevent the fear-inspired belief that we need to act NOW in spite of the costs. W. Edwards Deming proved decades ago that rework is expensive. The best economic approach is to do it right the first time, even if that means taking your time.

We save money by not spending on healthcare for pregnant women, but then we pay for years of healthcare of underweight babies for most of their lives - where's the savings? Short-term thinking is always more expensive in the long run.

We see the same shortsightedness in how we deal with education. The cost of an ignorant population who cannot think or even read is never factored in.

So if you are thinking that it is expensive to become sustainable, if you are hesitating to become a green business because of the cost, stop a minute and think about the expenses that are being externalized and passed on to future generations and then act in a way that makes the most economic sense - use ecological thinking.

Sustainable Business and the Seduction of Economics

Economics is all about choices. A sustainable business model is no less so, however there is considerable difference between the two.

Hewlett Packard was once a strong, proud company. They were leaders in their field of measurement. To be so required people with brains who were willing to explore and experiment and HP worked for years to create just such a culture. They attracted the brightest and best.

One of their core competencies was the ability to know the skills each person possessed and then connect those people quickly to address specific business needs. There was a time when a product idea could be discovered in China and within three months that product would be a reality. That was then.

Now HP makes its money on ink. The engineers are leaving and what is left are chemists. Yes they still make some technology products, but if money comes from ink, then the engineers and technicians no longer have the same cache. This means that people who have pride in their work as engineers will not go to HP where they would play second fiddle to chemists.

Humans are a meaning-making species. We need to feel that we add value. HP, by following the seduction of a strictly economic model is no longer adding value so decline is just a matter of time. Paul Krugman in the New York Times makes the same point. If we have a country of companies doing the same thing - chasing the shortsighted dollar (yes you CAN make money in the short-term) then we become a country of second-rate workers getting paid second-rate wages. Money actually follows brains - in the long term.

The seduction of economics is that we think of it as being about money, almost exclusively, but in economics there is NO discussion of value. There is a sort of assumption that the two are interrelated, and perhaps at one time that might have been true, but we are a clever people and our relentless pursuit of cash has hollowed out any interest in value, if there ever was one.

A sustainable business must be different. By understanding and working for long-term solutions and success, sustainable businesses seek to continuously add value. Every decision is made being cognizant of the value being created, of threats to that value, and of actions necessary to assure that value continues.

Horticulturists know that using synthetic fertilizers works. Plants grow large and look good - BUT - they become dependent upon that false nutrition and their roots become poorly developed so that they are incapable of getting their own nutrition from good soil. So a short-term economic seduction becomes a long-term economic loss because no lasting value was generated in the 'soil' of the economy.

Business grows in the soil of community. When it does not add value, then it becomes a parasite and the community weakens. We need to regain our pride in being human, with all of the incredible gifts that brings, and stop the dumbing down of our workforce, and our lives.

The planet has sustained itself for over 3.8 billion years by ensuring that ALL life contributes value to the whole. This is the goal of a truly sustainable, regenerative business!

Sustainable Economy - Oxymoron?

After the debacle of the bank bailout is thinking about a sustainable economy an oxymoron? We have a situation where institutions are rewarded for not adding value, where financial illiteracy runs the nation and belief trumps fact. University of California, Berkeley Professor Emmanuel Saez, in a paper, which covers data through 2007, points to a staggering, unprecedented disparity in American incomes. On his blog, Nobel prize-winning economist and *New York Times* columnist Paul Krugman called the numbers "truly amazing." Saez calculates that in 2007 the top .01 percent of American earners took home 6 percent of total U.S. wages, a figure that has nearly doubled since 2000. As of 2007, (the last year for which we have data) the top decile of American earners, Saez writes, pulled in 49.7 percent of total wages, a level that's higher than any other year since 1917 and even surpasses 1928, the peak of stock market bubble in the 'roaring 1920s." The middle class is disappearing.

Sounds bleak doesn't it? Tax rates for companies are at a historic low, with many multinational companies benefiting from tax havens and extensive loopholes. At the same time, the number of start-up companies is expanding, with new capital sources and a growing spirit of entrepreneurism. The debate over the appropriate role of government in regulating our market economy, and the extent to which the forces of the market are delivering benefits for the vast majority of citizens is also under review. Increasingly, companies are recognizing that it is a false choice to pit environmental stewardship against economic prosperity. As companies become more sustainable, there is a unique opening for the broader economy to follow suit. The economy remains highly dynamic, but traditional measurements of progress have become outdated and do not account for huge

WHAT'S IT MEAN – SHIFTING TO GREEN?

externalities in health care, the environment and other areas.

While the adoption of sustainability by individual companies (energy savings, supply chain, recycling and green business practices) is both commendable and important, it is not enough to bring about a new economy that truly values people as much as profit; that protects the value of natural resources for future use; and that creates healthy communities with vibrant economics. The continued practice of externalizing costs, subsidizing mature industries, and rewarding offshoring undermines the economic health of our internal economy.

Business has a major role to play in creating a New Economy that offers equity, transparency, strong domestic investment, tax fairness and product innovation based on sustainable business practices. Businesses like Interface Carpets, Inc. are leading the way by showcasing how competitiveness and profits can be increased, while being environmental stewards at the same time. Their record of cutting green house gas emissions by 82%, fossil fuel consumption by 60%, waste by 66%, water use by 75% while at the same time inventing and patenting new

165

machines, materials and manufacturing processes as they increased sales by 66%, doubled earnings and raised profit margins, is testimony to how effective a move toward sustainability can be. Not only have they saved money and made money, they have also achieved a 15% increase in employment!

Corporate Social Responsibility is not enough when companies must fight against ineffective or nonexistent governmental polices that make it impossible to obtain information (the Toxic Substances Control Act of 1976 has not been changed in 35 years) or that create unfair advantages (tax relief for businesses that use financial manipulation to shift their responsibilities to smaller companies and individual taxpayers).

The laws and regulations that guide our economy must promote sound, long-term decision-making, and they must take into account the externalities - social and environmental - that loom ever larger in influencing our national competitiveness and health. Given the shenanigans in Congress, do you think this is possible? If not, what do we do?

Final Thoughts

Externalizing costs is the single greatest threat to the creation of a strong and sustainably viable economy. Our shortsighted vision blinds us to the implications of our actions in ways that are both dangerous and ineffective.

∂

8 Resilience – a Sustainable Value

A child's world is fresh and new and beautiful, full of wonder and excitement. It is our misfortune that for most of us that clear-eyed vision, that true instinct for what is beautiful and awe-inspiring, is dimmed and even lost before we reach adulthood. ~ **Rachel Carson**

Sustainable Values

The Sustainable Values Set® is a collection of 15 values that act in concert with each other. They are tied together and if you enact one the others tag along naturally. That is absolutely true of the other value sets, but this one is newer so we have to be more conscious about enacting them all. Each value set has an emotional context: the Protective Value Set™ is fear; the Effective Value Set™ is a desire for success; and the Sustainable Values Set™ is appreciation and reverence. If the emotional context is maintained then the values fall naturally into focus, but if one of the other emotions creeps in, then so do those corresponding values, and if the coherence is lost then the result is corruption as none of the value set intents will be achieved.

Many people have had the experience where there was a high intent, but somehow things got scrambled and the results were not as expected. If you can think back, what was the emotional context? If you can remember, then check with the above and see what value set that emotion(s) best fits with. If you can do this, I'm willing to bet that the values that appeared were resonant with the emotions *but at odds with your intent.*

Authentically Resilient

I think resilience is key. It forms a major aspect of our values work. We elicit the values nature uses so successfully and apply them to leadership decision-making and business processes, enabling them to achieve resilience.

Resilience is neither simple nor easy, but the benefits are huge as so many other aspects of organizational life are affected. Nature is nothing if not resilient! She has supported Life on this planet for over 3.8 billion years. I've capitalized Life because one unaddressed aspect of Life on this planet is the Joy in just being alive. Yes there is struggle, but it is really just the thrill of being here that makes life such a kick.

That means for me, that a big part of being resilient is loving the process AND making sure that others are able to feel, express and contribute to that Joy as well. Think about it - do you enjoy coming to work? If companies can't get their job done in a manner in which everyone finds joy and fulfillment - what's the point?

We've been seduced into thinking that the joy will come. It will show up when we buy something new, when we pay that nagging bill, when we retire. We have been tricked into thinking that we can put joy off into the future somewhere if only we tolerate the current misery. That seduction is the enemy of resilience!

Trees LOVE being trees, flowers LOVE being flowers - that's one of the reasons we come away from being out in nature refreshed. Why should we GO to nature to be refreshed, why doesn't our own life refresh us? Maybe if we begin to act sustainably and LOVE being us, it will!

A Benefit of Sustainability - Resiliency

I was reading the Smithsonian's article *Faithful Monuments* by Jamie Katz and I got to pondering the benefits of sustainability to business. What triggered the thought was this quote:

"Ductility is the ability of the system to move back and forth, swell and shrink, and return to where it was in the beginning." by **Anthony Crosby** *a preservation architect for the Mission San Miguel.*

He was talking about preserving a building from earthquakes. The metaphor however, is a strong one for business. The changing landscape and the looming shifts in the ecological and economic stability of our society are certainly impacting business with more to come. That raised the question for me about whether sustainability would be an answer to the coming 'earthquakes.' Would a sustainable approach make a business more ductile?

The answer, is no. Here I want to make a crucial distinction between ductility and resilience. Being ductile is a good thing for a business, but it has a major shortcoming. The ability to move, to withstand the shaking and pummeling nature and our economic system are currently offering definitely enhances longevity. The ability to withstand growing and shrinking also makes a business more sustainable and even touches on the sustainable value of Dynamic Stability. So why did I say no?

The crucial difference is one that is fundamental to the difference between living and non-living systems. A distinction we often forget or gloss over. That difference is the ability to be *different* and still maintain integrity. In fact, for living systems, the ability to manage change, to learn and grow is *fundamental* to their integrity. And *that* is the difference between ductility and resilience.

Resilience provides for the skills and strength to withstand movement, growth and pruning, but a resilient organization, or a resilient person comes back from those experiences as a different being. It is not about snapping back to what existed before, but about embracing the new knowledge and experience and *being* different, changed, new, strong and with integrity after that experience.

For organizations it means that learning from nature, deeply understanding what makes nature resilient, *is* a method for remaining strong under adversity. Sustainability will most definitely help business through terrible and difficult times, but the business will not be the same afterwards - and that's a good thing.

❧

Final Thoughts

Ah, integrity. Can we be in integrity when we are not in harmony with the environment that nurtures us and makes our life possible? We hold ethics as the art and science of human relationships when, in reality it is the art and science of *relationships*. Only by including ALL life in our community and building authentic and respectful relationships with all other living things, can we be truly *in integrity* in our actions.

The interesting thing is that when we act with ALL Life in mind, then our human relationships radiate vitality as well.

&

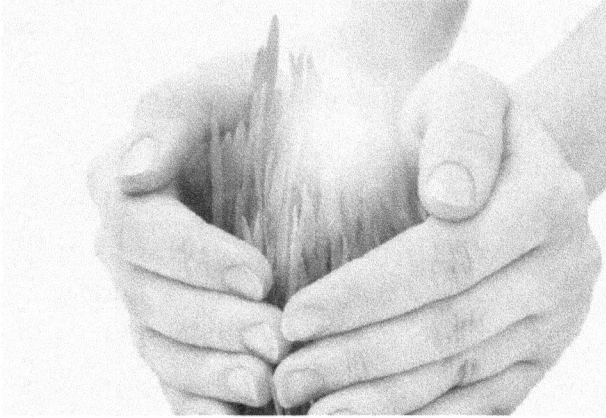

9 Six Steps To Making Your Company Sustainable

A man is ethical only when life, as such, is sacred to him, that of plants and animals as that of his fellow men, and when he devotes himself helpfully to all life that is in need of help.
~Albert Schweitzer

Making It Happen

This is an exploration about how business thinking changes in order to achieve true sustainability.

Green business matures as people begin thinking about what it means to be deep green by moving beyond a compliance focus. When I tell people that we take them beyond the wise use of energy, I get blank stares. What does it mean to "think like the Earth?" Going green, if you really mean deep green, is a strategy and not a tactic. Sustainability will change your organization forever, in ways you cannot anticipate, but the results will also go beyond your wildest dreams.

STEP ONE

Pick a framework. Having a coherent way of looking at the kind of changes you will be making helps everyone understand exactly what you are up to. An initial framework provides clarity in thinking about something very unfamiliar, while at the same time, giving everyone a shared language. As the journey progresses other frameworks may provide useful insights and once the company really 'gets it' you may develop your own approach integrating aspects of several of these frameworks.

The easiest and most common, but poorly understood framework is the Triple Bottom Line - People, Planet, Profit. The intent is that decisions should be made with these three in mind and in this order. In practice the people part has been interpreted as support for nonprofits that are working to rectify and remediate the global human rights issues brought on by our western lifestyle. The planet piece has been expressed by a strong commitment to reduced resource use. Profit becomes the tension point that drives innovation to achieve the other two *and* make sure the company is financially sound at the same time.

Natural Step has a framework that might help with understanding a bit more deeply what it means to recognize our impact on the Earth. The questions in these four areas drive that thinking:

What aspects of your organization contribute to an increased concentration of substances that are extracted from underground?

WHAT'S IT MEAN – SHIFTING TO GREEN?

What aspects of your company contribute to a concentration of substances that are created by humans?

What aspects of your company contribute to the degradation or abuse of natural systems?

What aspects of your organization contribute to the unequal distribution and use of the Earth's resources?

Additionally these thoughts can be very useful:

What benefits can be gained from the application of natural laws and principles to your business thinking and processes?

What values are needed to ensure a congruent leadership and a sustainably robust culture?

Adapted from The Natural Step for Business *by Brian Nattrass & Mary Altomare*

Another framework that some companies find useful is Biomimicry. This can be an eye opener, particularly for those companies that do a lot of product development and R&D in that area. This is the work of Janine Benyus as shared in her book, *Biomimicry*. The Biomimicry Institute and Guild have taken her work and expanded it considerably. The Biomimicry Life Principles are:

- Life creates the conditions conducive to life
- Adapt to changing conditions
- Be locally attuned and responsive
- Use life-friendly chemistry
- Be resource-efficient in material and energy
- Integrate development with growth
- Evolve to survive

There is depth to each of these that drive both a deeper understanding of nature and a sharper awareness of how to benefit from applying nature's approaches to every day problems.

Permaculture is another framework that has had profound revelations to companies that use it. Developed by Bill Mollison in 1978, - according to Wikipedia, the core tenets of permaculture are:

Care of the earth: Provision for all life systems to continue and multiply. This is the first principle, because without a healthy earth, humans cannot flourish.

Care of the people: Provision for people to access those resources necessary for their existence.

Return of Surplus: Reinvesting surpluses back into the system to provide for the first two ethics. This includes returning waste back into the system to recycle into usefulness.

And these are the principles:

Observe and interact: By taking time to engage with nature we can design solutions that suit our particular situation.

Catch and store energy: By developing systems that collect resources at peak abundance, we can use them in times of need.

Obtain a yield: Ensure that you are getting truly useful rewards as part of the work that you are doing.

Apply self-regulation and accept feedback: We need to discourage inappropriate activity to ensure that systems can continue to function well.

Use and value renewable resources and services: Make the best use of nature's abundance to reduce our consumptive behavior and dependence on non-renewable resources.

Produce no waste: By valuing and making use of all the resources that are available to us, nothing goes to waste.

Design from patterns to details: By stepping back, we can observe patterns in nature and society. These can form the backbone of our designs, with the details filled in as we go.

Integrate rather than segregate: By putting the right things in the right place, relationships develop between those things and they work together to support each other.

Use small and slow solutions: Small, slow systems are easier to maintain than big ones, making better use of local resources and producing more sustainable outcomes.

Use and value diversity: Diversity reduces vulnerability to a variety of threats and takes advantage of the unique nature of the environment in which it resides.

Use edges and value the marginal: The interface between things is where the most interesting events take place. These are often the most valuable, diverse and productive elements in the system.

Creatively use and respond to change: We can have a positive impact on inevitable change by carefully observing, and then intervening at the right time.

The last one I'll mention is the Sustainable Values Set®. This system was distilled as I combined Jane Jacobs's work on values as systems with the emerging understanding of how nature worked. This is a system of values that can act as a decision-making tool to ensure coherence and alignment throughout an organization. This system is one of three value systems that we use, mostly unconsciously, to make every day decisions. The interactions of these three systems are beyond this chapter, but understanding them is critical to ensure that emotions and old habits don't undermine our decision choices. Our assessments using these value systems are a groundbreaking approach to ethics in organizations.

The Sustainable Values Set®

To Achieve Commitment

- Integrity of the Whole
- All Actions Create the Conditions that Support Life
- Right Relationship
- Humans are Intrinsic to the Web of Life

II.   To Achieve Continuity

- Precautionary Principle
- Interdependency
- Optimization

III.   To Achieve Resilience

- Self-Organization
- Diversity
- Reciprocity
- Dynamic Stability

• Empowerment

IV. To Achieve Fertility/Innovation

• Co-Creation

• Ecologies

• Zero Waste

• Curiosity & Experimentation

Each of these frameworks has layers and layers of depth, each bringing more benefits. By creating a strategic plan you clarify your direction, and then the environmental plan will be assured to support that strategic direction. This is important to prevent backtracking and being tossed about by changing rules and regulations.

One of the major benefits of doing an environmental plan this way is that you can get ahead of the pack and make this journey an advantage in the marketplace. You end up ahead of changing compliance regulations as you can see where things are going. This means that you won't be caught by surprise or make major shifts at inopportune times. All of this saves time, money and morale!

The key to an effective sustainability effort is working to drive the change in thinking deep into the organization so everyone can help support the effort. When employees *get* what it means to *your* business to start working *with* the Earth there is a renewed commitment and energy that brings rewards of its own.

STEP TWO

The second step is closely allied with the normal first step for creating a green business, *energy conservation.* There are some differences however. Look around at your business practices and see what you use and what you do that has to do with things extracted from the earth. Oil is certainly one of those things, but what else do you use that is extracted? Metals, rare earth minerals (computers, cell phones), sand (concrete), coal, limestone, marble, etc. - you get the drift.

Pay particular attention if they accumulate on the surface during processing and/or after use. The trick is to use these kinds of substances at the same rate they are replenished. I hope that gives you pause. Many of these substances have taken millions of years to form, and that's the point. If we continue to use them faster than they are replenished, then they are finite and we will run out.

If we are and continue to be dependent upon materials that are finite then we run the risk of increased price and a catastrophe when they are finally depleted or too costly to continue to use.

This is a key understanding about sustainability. Act NOW before the situation is dire by finding substitutes, creating alternatives or changing your processes to not need these materials. By getting ahead of the curve you can lead the market by creating cost efficiencies before others in your industry. This gives you more time and many more opportunities than those who wait until the last minute will have.

Our strategic planning process can roll right over into creating an environmental plan that helps you deal with these kinds of questions. As you get clear on where you are going, you will also see what aspects of your business are important to look at from a sustainability lens. You will be able to prioritize and know how to leverage your resources and develop your timeline without being distracted. Starting early really puts you ahead of the game!

STEP THREE

Make the shift to sustainable leadership. This is not easy and may well be the most difficult step. Without shifting to sustainable leadership, the rest of the journey will be very much harder and the likelihood of completing the journey almost nonexistent. Resource reduction can be delegated and authorized. That is not the best way, but improving your record keeping and changing habits (turning off lights and computers) do not demand as much engagement as simply obedience.

As things get more complicated everyone has to be on the same page. Now I know you've heard this phrase before, but this is a literal truth, not a figurative one. This is the holy grail of management and has been for over 60 years. So far few companies have achieved it and those that do are legendary. Yet to address – even to find – the myriads of issues that make our companies unsustainable takes the eyes, ears and minds of all employees at all levels. A command and control leadership style won't cut it!

Not only does everyone have to be on board, they have to have the responsibility and the authority to act to address issues as they find them. This does not mean everyone is acting independently, but that there is trust with processes in place to ensure everyone knows what everyone else is doing. All employees have to learn together and share what they are discovering. That means that there are structures and procedures in place to make that possible. This is change on steroids.

Sustainable leadership requires a passion for sustainability, a deep love of the Earth, and a consistent commitment for the long haul. A sustainable leader is worthy of trust and trusts others as well. If employees don't think they are trusted you will not get the kinds of creative and intelligent risk behavior you need to leap into new areas that are deemed necessary. Taking the time to find new suppliers or to even support the development of new suppliers is a very different game from just switching.

Sustainable leaders need to understand and practice systems thinking as well as be able to teach it. They need to be learners by modeling learning for their organization. They need to be cheerleaders and people developers, facilitating the growth of their workforce in the same ways

189

they themselves are growing. Sustainable leaders need to be comfortable with ambiguity and flexible so that continuous change is consistently supported. Most of all, sustainable leaders need to be humble and forgiving. This is a task no one can do alone, and as the ways we have said 'no' to life rise to the surface, forgiveness becomes the path to freedom.

STEP FOUR

Zero Waste. Now things get serious. In nature there is no waste. Nature functions as a closed system with everything being reused. We are the only species that withholds from nature and we do that with a vengeance. From a business perspective, no waste means that whatever is not used can be *and is* used by someone else. Waste Management took this on and has learned to create alliances to take and reuse many of the things we throw away. Now we all need to learn that. There are cases where this is currently impossible, as we haven't invented the alternative. Interface Carpets sponsored development and invention when they ran into many of those circumstances.

Pursuing zero waste is a game changer. Thinking this way becomes a major push for innovation, with the resulting benefits of better products, new products, a wider net of alliances, new revenue streams and the list goes on. It is here that the real lasting benefits of becoming sustainable start to show themselves.

Gunter Pauli and his Blue Economy organization showcases inventions stemming from this approach, and the Zero Organization works to show us how it can be done. His goal of taking 10 years to create 100 inventions that will generate 100 million jobs is living proof of the astounding benefits both short and long-term that comes from a zero waste approach.

STEP FIVE

Culture change. By now it should be clear why everyone needs to be passionately involved and free to contribute. This requires a very strong, disciplined and empowered culture. This is not something that happens overnight, so it starts as soon as the leadership begins their own journey into the sustainable model. Learning to trust others is not something that happens overnight and all too often "trust" is seen as not paying attention. It is easier to ignore what's going on than to check in, support and teach. We all too often fail to ask probing questions as 'proof' that we trust. This is blind faith as real trust encourages questioning with the corresponding honest answers. Trust develops (it's a two way street) when bad things happen and people are still treated with respect. Trust doesn't mean that people are infallible; it means that they can and will make things good; if or when bad things happen.

Communication is one of the biggest reasons there is little trust in most organizations. Not having processes in place to make sure people are notified in a timely fashion, being secretive, not taking the time to actually talk with people are all simple acts that can go a long way in generating trust, if they are dealt with correctly. Allowing, even encouraging deep questioning goes a very long way in developing trust.

Shifting from a punitive approach to mistakes to a learning one is the other very simple change that will make a culture not only more resilient, but more engaged and innovative. When conditions are created that allow for transparency in decision-making and the sharing of learning when things don't turn out as expected, then the impossible becomes possible!

STEP SIX

Becoming Regenerative. Just as in the wild, effective change requires that all participants co-evolve. As the organization begins to understand and live the chosen framework, new insights into what needs to shift and how begin to percolate. Following the lead of Mother Nature can open up new and unusual opportunities. As the framework becomes a reality wonderful and curious things can happen.

My favorite story is that of Interface Carpets, Inc. When Ray Anderson was driven to take on sustainability by his employees his search led him to Paul Hawkins' book *The Ecology of Commerce.* This opened his eyes to the role of business in the destruction of our world. It gave him the fire and dedication to bring that lesson home to his small carpet factory and over the past 17 years Ray's company has been able to achieve: a cut in greenhouse gas emissions of 82%; a cut in fossil fuel consumption of 60%; a cut in waste of 66%; a cut in water use of 75%, and they have invented & patented new machines, materials &

manufacturing processes; increased sales by 66%; doubled earnings; increased profit margins and plan to be carbon neutral by 2020. All this from a small manufacturer who was committed to making business the solution instead of the problem. They are on the path to regeneration – to making their business practices enhance the wellbeing of nature!

The company, as it exists today, is very different from the company that started this journey! They have evolved in ways they could not have predicted and they did so by committing to let nature lead.

Final Thoughts

That's it. As you can see there are only six steps, they are not easy and they won't happen fast, but the change will be profound, your business will benefit in ways you can't even imagine and the key to success with the change is *you*, so you had better start now!

10 The Future – a Possibility?

What is really amazing and frustrating is mankind's habit of refusing to see the obvious and inevitable, until it is there, and then muttering about unforeseen catastrophes. ~**Isaac Asimov**

Back to the Future?

The future is always in the distant time that is yet to come. It is a 'someday' concept. It is something we talk about, but know that it isn't real and with all of the changes we've seen in the past 100 years (my father's lifetime), something we know we can't know. Yet now, something's changed. The future is *here*. The changes we have been talking about for the past 50-60 years are now happening - they are no longer just speculation.

The parts per million of carbon have reached 400 for the first time in recorded history. We have no clear idea what this will mean for life, however we do have some indication of the issues we might face. The warming of the planet - 2 degrees, 4 degrees, doesn't sound so bad. We forget that most life forms on this planet live within a rather narrow temperature range. As humans we have been able to extend that range and with our artificial methods we have expanded it even further. However consider how you feel when your temperature is 100 degrees – only 2 degrees warmer. Not too good, right? What happens when your temperature reaches 102? This is what the Earth is going through and the prognosis is that her temperature will go even higher. In fact this fast of an acceleration of temperature has never before been experienced in the history of the planet, as far as we know, so the actual impact is quite unknown.

So the question of the future is very much just that – a question.

CAN we meet our needs and those of the future?

Brundtland Commission of the United Nations on March 20, 1987 declared: "sustainable development is development that meets the needs of the present without compromising the ability of future generations to meet their own needs. This is the most commonly used definition. Their report, 26 years ago determined that: **Sustainability** is the capacity to endure. For humans, sustainability is the long-term maintenance of wellbeing, which has environmental, economic, and social dimensions, and encompasses the concept of stewardship, the responsible management of resource use. In ecology, sustainability describes how biological systems remain diverse and productive over time, a necessary precondition for human wellbeing. Long-lived and healthy wetlands and forests are examples of sustainable biological systems.

Healthy ecosystems and environments provide vital goods and services to humans and other organisms. There are two major ways of managing human impact on ecosystem services: One approach is environmental management - this approach is based largely on information gained from earth science, environmental science and conservation biology. Another approach is management of consumption of resources, which is based largely on information gained from economics.

Human sustainability interfaces with economics through the social and ecological consequences of economic activity. Moving towards sustainability is also a social challenge that entails among other factors, international and national law, urban planning and transport, local and individual lifestyles and ethical consumerism. Ways of living more sustainably can take many forms from reorganizing living conditions (e.g. eco-villages, eco-municipalities and sustainable cities), to reappraising work practices (e.g. using permaculture, green building, sustainable agriculture) or developing new technologies that reduce the consumption of resources. (According to the Wikipedia).

How far have we come in 26years? Most of us have some familiarity with budgeting. If I want to make a big expenditure in the future (for a vacation, say) then I need to curtail my spending now to save money for that event. All of us have experience with forgoing something now for a nicer something in the future. That in essence, is what the Brundtland report recommended. How are we doing?

More to the point, what have YOU given up lately? What organization, what company do you know of that has chosen to stop expansion or that has even chosen to flatten its growth to current levels? What company do you know that has chosen to limit its budget to current levels?

Easter Island seemed to have this same problem and look where it got them. Cutting down the last tree didn't save, but doomed them (what was left of them) to a meager and poverty stricken existence. Hmmm, what do you think we've learned since then? How strong is our will power to ensure the existence, let alone lifestyle of

future generations given that we'd have to limit
our own immediate lifestyle? Easter Island
survived because of outside influence (Chile).
Where are we going to find outside support?

Creating a Sustainable Future

If you have been reading this book you
know I'm a sustainability geek. Today however, I
want to talk about an article I read of all places, in
Sunset Magazine. It is so progressive I actually
thought I was reading FastCompany.

One of the things Obama has tried to do
was to rethink our transportation infrastructure.
This is not about politics (really) it's about
reducing energy use and trying to get ahead of our
travel needs. We are a big country and one of the
lures of the automobile is the ability to get
anywhere we want to go easily and quickly. At
least it used to be that way.

Having been in Europe and used their
trains to get around, I have to say I came home
wondering what was wrong with us. I haven't
been to Japan, but I can speculate about an
experience on their trains. We only use trains to

move stuff - mostly. Amtrack is a shadow of its former self and hardly a robust image of what it could be.

So it is with some consternation that I watched several Republican governors, in misguided political angst, refuse money for train and light rail development. They effectively thwarted a rather grand concept that was very poorly sold, to link major parts of the country together. This would have made it easy and quick to reach parts of the country that actually want to connect. Too bad!

The article in Sunset titled The Future of Train Travel was amazing (it doesn't seem to be available online). The train stations had what you would expect in terms of solar panels and hydraulic table, but it also had hydroponic gardens so you could pick your own fresh salad, and citrus trees to provide oranges and juice, but what was more amazing and what really got me thinking was their 'fantasy car' approach.

They had an Adventure Car for the sports enthusiast, an Ultra Wired Car that included an Apple Store Genius bar and white board, and a Pet Car where you could get your pet groomed.

WHAT'S IT MEAN – SHIFTING TO GREEN?

Now that's thinking out of the box. Doesn't your mind just go off? What other kinds of cars can you visualize? Send me some of your ideas; I'd love to hear them!

Being sustainable doesn't have to be boring or stuffy. It can be and needs to be fun! For me it is inspiring and exciting as my mind gets filled with new possibilities and old problems get solved and issues disappear and challenges are surmounted. That's why I'm a sustainable geek, oh and yes; I do love the planet too.

Final Thoughts

In the past few years the income gap has gotten greater. The middle class is struggling to just stay afloat. Wages have plateaued at 1970 levels. People are working so hard just to keep up that thinking about the things in this book is out of the question. We are so burdened by everyday pressures that thinking about and acting for the future seems immediately unimportant.

Firefighting and jumping from one crisis to another does not make for a well-planned future. In truth, planning never makes the future, but it makes the transition from here to there a bit easier. When we are under pressure decision-making is often made with short-term goals in mind and driven by the most immediate and pressing needs. Our noble intentions and deepest desires can get lost in the shuffle. It is here that the Sustainable Values Set® can shine. It allows for coherence in a fragmented world and consistency when we are buffeted by circumstance.

How and when will you take the time to act as if the future you desired is real, here and now? Learning and applying the recommendations in this short work will help indeed! Use the resources in the End Notes and call us, if you want to explore personal and organizational growth opportunitites.

ॐ

A Call to Action

I'm looking to work with companies that resonate with the ideas put forth in this book. If you are such a company, please get in touch – together we can recreate our world! Get in touch by calling 303-818-4147 or 866-872-8623 or by email at ethicalimpact@gmail.com.

࿐

AN OFFER JUST FOR YOU

What Drives Culture?

Learn about the four kinds of culture and the leadership that creates them. Discover the benefits and challenges in each and how that impacts your approach to sustainability. Best of all find out how to create the culture that works for you in developing a sustainable business.

Using the code: NATURE enables you to get the $75 webinar for only $25 a $50 saving!

Visit
http://whatsitmeanshiftingtogreen.com/culture

ൟ

ABOUT THE AUTHOR

Kathryn Alexander, MA is an author, speaker and culture coach working with people desiring to create organizations that foster work environments promoting creativity, personal initiative and meaningful participation. She excels at helping leaders and teams create and navigate their desired future.

In her 16 years working with change, in organizations ranging from start-ups to Fortune 50 companies, she has learned the secret that effective organizations are ethical organizations. Working with leaders and teams to address the need to *think differently* about their problems, she has been instrumental in co-creating significant shifts in her client companies.

Kathryn has an MA in Organizational Development and Transformation and was recognized as the Business Woman of the Year by the Boulder Chapter of the Business and Professional Women, and Women *to Watch in Sustainability* by the Boulder, Colorado Westword in 2012.

All photographs of Kathryn are courtesy of Marge Maago.

☙

End Notes

HOW SHOULD WE LIVE

1 David Blackmon Article

http://www.forbes.com/sites/davidblackmon/2013/07/01/water-for-fracking-in-context/

2 Forbes

http://www.forbes.com/

3 Ceres

http://www.forbes.com/companies/ceres/

4 Interface Carpets, Inc.

http://www.interfaceglobal.com

5 Zeri

http://www.zeri.org/ZERI/Case_Studies.html

6 Grupo Balbo

http://www.sustainablebusiness.com/index.cfm/go/news.printerfriendly/id/22906

CHAPTER ONE

1 Chasing Ice

http://www.chasingice.com/

2 She's Alive

http://www.youtube.com/watch?v=nGeXdv-uPaw

3 Walter J. Stahel

http://www.youtube.com/watch?v=PhJ-YZwDAVo

4 Satyana Institute

http://satyana.org/

5 Hooked on Growth

http://youtube.com/watchh?r=AYrrnywWvic

6 Thomas Berry

http://www.thomasberry.org/

CHAPTER TWO

1 Happy Planet Index

http://www.happyplanetindex.org

2 Flock of Birds Video

http://youtube/M1Q-EbX6dso

3 Peggy Holman

http://peggyholman.com

4 Engaging Emergence

http://amazon.com/engaging-emergence-turning-upheaval-opportunity/dp/1605095214

5 Margaret Wheatley

http://www.margaretwheatley.com

6 Berkana Institute

http://berkana.org

7 Life Cycle of Emergence

http://berkana.org/berkana_articles/lifecycle-of-emergence-using-emergence-to-take-social-innovation-to-scale/

8 City of Kalundborg, Denmark

http://biy.ly/M3XKQl

9 Machu Picchu

http://architecturalmoleskin.blogspot.com/2011/05/m
avhu-picchu-aspects-of-engineering.html

10 Emotions in the Workplace

http://hvm.sagepub.com/content/48/2/97.short

CHAPTER THREE

1 Brian Nattrass

http://www.newsociety.com/Contributors/N/Nattrass-
Brian

2 Mary Altomare

http://www.newsociety.com/Contributors/A/Altomare
-Mary

3 Hartwick Forest

http://www.michigandnr.com/parksandtrails/Details.as
px?type=SPRK&id=453

4 Trees and Crime

http://actrees.org/site/resources/research/the_effect_o
f_trees_on_crime_in_portland_oreg.php

5 Grand Canyon Mines

http://action.biologicaldiversity.org/p/dia/action/publi
c/?action_KEY=6027&tag=gcjul2011

6 Pebble Mine

http://www.takepart.com/article/2013/04/30/pebble-
mine-alaska-damage-streams-salmon-epa-decides

CHAPTER FIVE

1 Triplepundit

http://www.triplepundit.com/2009/09/building-an-
organizational-culture-of-sustainability-employee-
engagement/

2 Network for Business Sustainability

http://www.nbs.net/knowledge/culture/systematic-
review-organizational-culture/

3 Boston Corporate Citizenship Conference

http://www.bcccc.net/index.cfm%3FpageId=2200

4 Boston Corporate Citizenship Projects

http://www.bcccc.net/index.cfm?pageId=2244

5 Gross National Happiness Index

http://grossnationalhappinessindex.com/articles/

CHAPTER SIX

1 Michael Watkins

http://www.google.com/url?sa=t&rct=j&q=&esrc=s&s
ource=web&cd=2&ved=0CC4QFjAB&url=http%3A%2
F%2Fwww.transfieldworley.com.au%2Ficms_docs%2F1
15408_Transition_Management_and_the_Actual_Costs_
of_Change.pdf&ei=YFh2U8PQGtePqAam5ICgBw&usg
=AFQjCNFdSs3k8ymSPkL8EhuEhHhObInExA&bvm
=bv.66699033,d.b2k

2 Sustainable Leadership

http://whatsitmeanshiftingtogreen.com/leadership

3 Japan's Tsunami

http://nyti.ms/ih9G7s

4 Earth Pictures

http://bit.ly/lLbkIR

CHAPTER SEVEN

1 Creating Alternative Futures

http://www.goodreads.com/book/show/2018469.Creating_Alternative_Future

2 Cradle to Cradle

http://www.mcdonough.com/speaking-writing/cradle-to-cradle/

3 Ann Charles

http://www.fastcompany.com/1744749/to-create-a-true-csr-culture-you-have-to-start-with-wallstreet?partner=rss&utm_source=API&utm_medium=twitter

4 Fast Company

http://www.fastcompany.com/

5 Capitalist's Paradox

http://blogs.hbr.org/haque/2011/03/the_capitalists_paradox.html

6 Sustainable Capitalism

http://www.sustainablecapitalism.org/

7 Conscious Capitalism

http://www.consciouscapitalism.org/index.html

8 Decontaminating Fukushima

http://www.foxnews.com/world/2011/04/11/reports-japan-decides-raise-nuclear-crisis-alert-level-7-highest-equal/ - ixzz1JHQ70Eob

9 Conscious Capitalism Institute

http://www.cc-institute.com/cci/

10 Hewlett Packard

http://www.bloomberg.com/news/2013-02-21/hewlett-packard-forecast-tops-estimates-on-data-center-sales.html

11 Paul Krugman

http://en.wikipedia.org/wiki/Paul_Krugman

12 Paul Krugman in the NY Times

http://www.nytimes.com/2011/03/07/opinion/07krugman.html?ref=paulkrugman

13 Fertilizer Plant Damage

http://www.ehow.com/info_7774072_inorganic-fertilizers-burning-plant-roots.html

14 Income Disparity

http://elsa.berkeley.edu/%7Esaez/

15 Paul Krugman on Income Disparity

http://krugman.blogs.nytimes.com/2009/08/13/even-more-gilded/

16 Interface Carpets Global, Inc.

http://www.interfaceglobal.com/Sustainability.aspx

17 Toxic Substances Control Act 1976

http://en.wikipedia.org/wiki/Toxic_Substances_Control_Act_of_1976

CHAPTER NINE

1 Natural Step

http://www.naturalstep.org/usa

2 Natural Step for Business

http://www.newsociety.com/Books/N/The-Natural-Step-for-Business

3 Biomimicry

http://biomimicry.net

4 Permaculture Guild

http://www.permacultureguild.org

5 Bill Mollison

http://www.abc.net.au/rural/legends/stories/4_1.htm

6 Sustainable Value Set®

http://whatsitmeanshiftingtogreen.com/Products/

7 Leadership Cultural Assessment

http://whatsitmeanshiftingtogreen.com/Products/

8 Blue Economy

http://www.theblueeconomy.org/blue/Home.html

9 Zero Organization (Zeri)

http://www.zeri.org/ZERI/Home.html

CHAPTER TEN

1 Carbon Measure

http://climate.nasa.gov/400ppmquotes

2 Definition of Sustainability

http://en.wikipedia.org/wiki/Sustainability

3 Easter Island

http://www.netaxs.com/~trance/rapanui.html

4 Sunset Magazine

http://www.sunset.com/magazine/current-issue/

5 Fast Company

http://www.fastcompany.com/

FINAL THOUGHTS

1 Plateaued Wages

http://www.washingtonpost.com/blogs/wonkblog/wp/
2012/07/31/wages-arent-stagnating-theyre-plummeting/

www.ingramcontent.com/pod-product-compliance
Lightning Source LLC
Chambersburg PA
CBHW031928190326
41519CB00007B/450